CANADIAN PACIFIC
RAILWAY

TOM MURRAY

Voyageur Press

Dedication

This book is dedicated to my wife, Marcia,
who has given me a life that makes projects like this one possible.

First published in 2006 by Voyageur Press, an imprint of MBI Publishing Company, Galtier Plaza, Suite 200, 380 Jackson Street, St. Paul, MN 55101-3885 USA

MBI titles are also available at discounts in bulk quantity for industrial or sales-promotional use. For details write to Special Sales Manager at MBI Publishing Company, Galtier Plaza, Suite 200, 380 Jackson Street, St. Paul, MN 55101-3885 USA.

ISBN-13: 978-0-7603-2255-0
ISBN-10: 0-7603-2255-4

Edited by Dennis Pernu
Designed by Christopher Fayers

Front cover: CP 9644 leads eastbound Train 874 on the Swift Current Subdivision at Parkbeg, Saskatchewan, in September 1998. The train is carrying metallurgical coal from Line Creek, British Columbia, to Chicago. *John Leopard*

Frontis: A 1947 advertisement touts Canadian Pacific as a one-stop source for all of the traveler's summer vacation arrangements.

Title pages: CP 5499, leading westbound Train 957 at Macklin, Saskatchewan, on the Hardisty Subdivision in September 1998, was originally a Union Pacific unit, rebuilt in 1995 as an SD40M-2. The Hardisty Subdivision, running between Hardisty and Wilkie, serves as part of a secondary main line across Saskatchewan, north of CPR's primary route through Moose Jaw. *John Leopard*

Back cover: The westbound Canadian departs Field, British Columbia, at the foot of the Big Hill, while on the next track Train 902 waits to depart eastbound behind SD40-2 5671. Field was named after U.S. industrialist Cyrus Field and was the location of Mount Stephen House, one of CPR's early dining and lodging facilities, which was demolished in 1954. *Steve Patterson*

Inset: Few railroads could compete with the spectacular scenery experienced aboard *The Canadian* while traversing the Rockies.

Printed in China

CONTENTS

ACKNOWLEDGMENTS

To be given an opportunity to write about Canadian Pacific Railway is a great privilege. It is, justifiably, one of the best-documented companies in North America, and my bookshelves have been groaning under the weight of the books written by others about its history. I am grateful to all of them for providing material for me to draw on. I hope that readers who are not already familiar with these earlier books will be motivated, after reading this one, to dig deeper. References to several of these works are found in the text of this book, and the bibliography contains a fuller list.

Generations of photographers have trained their lenses on CPR. This made for such an abundance of archival and contemporary photos that it was a great challenge to choose the ones to appear here. I did my best to select photos that are both visually appealing and as representative as possible of the company's history and geography. I am indebted to all ten of the photographers who allowed their material to be reproduced in this book: Bruce Blackadar, Eric Blasko, John Leopard, Bill Linley, Phil Mason, Steve Patterson, George Pitarys, Jim Shaughnessy, Stan Smaill, and Pat Yough.

CPR was constructed at a time when photography was already well developed as a commercial enterprise, and technical advancements had made it possible to take photographs in the field (even under adverse conditions). The building of the railway was an event of national importance in Canada, and its early years were amply recorded. I want to thank the Glenbow Archives in Calgary and Library and Archives Canada in Ottawa, both of which provided archival photos for this book.

The California State Railroad Museum allowed the use of several photographs by Philip R. Hastings, M.D., whose collection was donated to the museum by his family in 1997. The Denver Public Library's Western History Collection, which is the custodian of the Otto C. Perry Memorial Collection of Railroad Photographs, allowed three of Mr. Perry's CPR photos to be reproduced here.

Although CPR's history has been well documented, it's possible for a writer to go astray, and to reduce that potential I had assistance from several railway veterans. Raymond L. Kennedy, who was a longtime CPR employee, provided detailed feedback on an early draft of this book and saved me from several errors. F. H. Howard, who had a long career in the Canadian transportation industry, reviewed the text and gave me the benefit of his experiences with the people of CPR. Former Canadian Pacific Chairman and Chief Executive Officer (and fourth-generation CPR employee) William W. Stinson provided a number of helpful notes and comments on the draft text. CPR veterans Phil Mason and Stan Smaill, both of whom provided photos for this book, also gave me a great deal of help in understanding the history of this company.

Despite the assistance of such knowledgeable people, errors of fact and interpretation may have found their way into this book. They are my responsibility alone.

Finally, I have been fortunate to have the support of my wife, Marcia, who has not only enabled me to devote time to this project but has actively encouraged it. For that reason, and many others, this book is dedicated to her.

INTRODUCTION

Canadian Pacific began as a railway, became a global transportation system, and then evolved into a diversified industrial conglomerate. Today it is, once again, a railway. This book is an effort to tell the story not just of the railway, but of the company that was created around it.

That story is a rich one, with many colorful individuals involved. They include George Stephen and Donald Smith, cousins from Scotland whose vision made Canadian Pacific possible; William Cornelius Van Horne, a gifted railroader who guided the company through its perilous years of construction and early operation; Thomas Shaughnessy, an administrative and logistical wizard who strengthened the railway both physically and financially; Edward Beatty, who helped the company survive the challenges of vigorous competition and demoralizing economic conditions; Norris Crump, an up-from-the-ranks railroader who forced the company to change technologically and spurred its expansion into new lines of business; and Ian Sinclair, who alienated many by his emphasis on non-rail enterprises, but whose instincts may well have been the right ones, given the economic and regulatory climate of his time.

As a railway, CPR has long had a reputation for conservatism, for not spending a dollar that was not absolutely necessary. That reputation is no accident. Its roots are in the financial challenges that faced the company throughout its early years, as it pushed across Canada, through inhospitable

An eastbound freight powered by five SD40 and SD40-2 locomotives makes its way along the Kicking Horse River on CPR's Mountain Subdivision in August 1977. The train has just left Golden, British Columbia. *Bruce Blackadar*

territory. There were no footsteps for the railway's builders to follow in, and no way to know in advance what physical challenges they would face. As the line was extended westward, the early estimates of construction costs proved over-optimistic. The fact that CPR has survived as an independent company since its incorporation in 1881 without going through bankruptcy (in an industry where corporate reorganizations have been commonplace) is testimony to the merits of its fiscal prudence.

But being tight with a dollar did not make Canadian Pacific the company that it became—one whose impact on the national life of Canada has been beyond measure. One generation of CPR leaders after another has taken an expansive view of the company's capabilities and potential, beginning with George Stephen, who saw the railway as the cornerstone of an enterprise that would link Britain and Asia. It has never been a company that shied away from new opportunities.

For a railway, geography is destiny. In February 2006, CPR observed the 125th anniversary of its incorporation. Although the company has radically changed in terms of technology, operating practices, and traffic during that time, its geography remains much the same as when it was completed

The rear brakeman has left the caboose and is getting into position to help yard his train as it arrives at the Tadanac Yard near Trail, British Columbia, in October 1972. This was a scene that would soon become obsolete as railroads eliminated roofwalks from freight cars in the interest of safety. Cabooses, too, would be phased out in the coming years. *Tom Murray*

across Canada in 1885. Every day, CPR faces challenges that George Stephen and William Van Horne would understand, as its employees move trains over Kicking Horse Pass, keep the railway operating in inclement weather on the north shore of Lake Superior, and serve the transportation needs of farmers on the Canadian prairie.

Before beginning the story, a note on style is in order. In this book, the abbreviation "CPR" is generally used to refer to the company. In conversation, and in many prior books, common practice has been to refer to "the CPR" or "the C.P.R." However, in company publications (such as annual reports)

today's Canadian Pacific Railway Limited refers to itself as "CPR." This is in line with the practice of other contemporary railroads. However, in train operations and on freight cars and other equipment, the shorter "CP" is generally used as an abbreviation or reporting mark. Therefore, in photo captions the reader will often find "CP" used, as in "engine CP 4105" or "extra CP 5856 west." In other places, the abbreviation "CP" is used in connection with the company's non-rail activities.

Also, the reader should be aware that Canadian Pacific Railway Limited did not sponsor this book, or participate in its development.

The towers of Canada's Parliament buildings can be seen in the background at Ottawa Union Station in June 1965. Vancouver-Montreal Train 8, *The Dominion*, behind CP FP7 1431, is completing its station stop. This train carries a heavy load of express and mail in addition to its passenger business. Next to it is Ottawa-Montreal Train 232. *Bill Linley*

CHAPTER ONE

A Railway to Create a Nation

Most North American railroads began their lives as local or regional

enterprises, growing larger over time through acquisition and new con-

struction. By contrast, Canadian Pacific Railway was conceived from

the beginning as transcontinental in scope. This railway would not

only provide transportation, but would also give tangible expression to

the political, economic, and social connections between Canada's east-

ern and western provinces. The history of Canadian Pacific is, in many

ways, the history of Canada itself.

The building of a railway across Canada was motivated largely by political considerations. In the United States, anti-British sentiment increased during the Civil War, and in British North America there was fear that the north-south trade on which the provinces depended would disappear. Following the United States' purchase of Alaska from Russia, there was talk among some U.S. politicians of the unification of all North American lands bordering the Pacific Ocean, or even the annexation of all the lands north of the border.

British North America, was, until 1867, a loose amalgamation of provinces. To forestall the annexation of British Columbia and other British territory by the Americans, a stronger form of union was needed. Confederation was the answer.

The first provinces to unite as Canada in 1867 were Ontario, Quebec, Nova Scotia, and New Brunswick, followed by Manitoba in 1870. While they continued to have differences politically and economically, these provinces did at least represent a contiguous territory with many common interests.

Bringing British Columbia into Confederation was more complicated. Prior to 1868, the Hudson's Bay Company controlled the central part of British North America, thus interposing a privately controlled region between east and west. The passage of the Rupert's Land Act in that year removed this obstacle but did nothing to mitigate the physical barriers between the Atlantic and Pacific regions.

By 1870, political forces within British Columbia had reached agreement on the terms under which they would agree to Confederation, and a delegation traveled to Ottawa to negotiate with the government of Canada. The agreement that emerged included a promise by Canada that a railway would be built to link British Columbia with the East. Construction was to begin within two years and completion was promised within ten years. Following ratification of the

deal by provincial and Canadian legislatures, British Columbia became part of Canada on July 19, 1871.

A railway across Canada would never have been built were it not for the vision and commitment of Sir John A. Macdonald, leader of the Conservative Party, who served as prime minister of Canada from 1867 to 1873 and from 1878 until his death in 1891. He spearheaded the confederation movement, and he understood the importance of a railway in uniting the nation.

Government subsidies would be critical in getting the railway built, since it would tap into lands that had no economic activity beyond fur trading. As John Lorne McDougall writes in *Canadian Pacific: A Brief History*, "Canadian Pacific came into existence at the time and in the shape it did because it was an answer to a basic national problem and because the government was, for that reason, ready to provide the subsidies for it. It was essential to the life of Canada as a nation, but in economic terms it was a desperately premature enterprise."

Macdonald's eagerness to get the railway built was largely responsible for the gap in his career as prime minister from 1873 to 1878. In the months prior to British Columbia's entry into Canada, Macdonald encouraged shipping magnate and industrialist Hugh Allan, then Canada's richest man, to form an enterprise to build the railway.

At this time, many believed that an all-Canada route between east and west was

The last rays of sun hit the peaks of the Sir Donald Range as a westbound coal train passes Glacier, British Columbia, having just exited the Connaught Tunnel in November 1977. Photographer Mason notes, "The peaks visible in the photo are, left to right, Eagle Peak and Mount Uto and the flank of Mount Sir Donald, visible on the right. The summit of the Rogers Pass grade is about mid-train." The mountain and the range are named after Sir Donald Smith, a founder of Canadian Pacific. *Phil Mason*

impractical due to the rugged nature of the land north of Lake Superior. American railroaders were confident that a route that dipped into the U.S. would be the only way of connecting the eastern provinces with British Columbia. Even the management of Canada's largest railway, the Grand Trunk,

shared this view; Grand Trunk steered clear of any involvement in transcontinental railway projects until the twentieth century.

This view matched well with the self-interest of the owners and operators of U.S. railroads in the northern states, from the Great Lakes westward. One of those was Northern Pacific's banker, Jay Cooke. In December 1871, Cooke and other Americans, with Hugh Allan as the sole Canadian member, formed a partnership to build the Canada Pacific Railway. They did not disclose publicly that the railway would be routed through Sault Ste. Marie, Ontario, and then across the Upper Peninsula of Michigan and northern Wisconsin to a connection with the Northern Pacific at Duluth, Minnesota.

The lack of Canadian representation made this proposal politically unacceptable, and in February 1873 a new company, to be known as Canadian Pacific Railway Company, was formed. Allan was its president, it was Canadian in character, and it was specifically chartered to run north of Lake Superior.

However, this enterprise was doomed by the disclosure of Allan's prior dealings with Cooke and the other Americans. The fact that Macdonald had encouraged the Allan group (even though he was not aware of their planned route via the United States) gave the Liberal opposition in Parliament the fuel they needed to bring Macdonald down. The resulting furor became known as the Pacific Scandal. Faced with mounting criticism over his distribution of money from Allan to Conservative candidates, Macdonald resigned on November 5, 1873.

Historian W. Kaye Lamb, in his book *History of the Canadian Pacific Railway*, describes the outcome of the scandal: "Denied financial backing, the first Canadian Pacific Railway Company quietly disappeared. Sir Hugh Allan withdrew from the Pacific railway scene, and the threat of an American takeover disappeared."

In 1885, CPR construction crews building from the east reached Revelstoke, British Columbia, on the Columbia River. A set of three SD402F units leads a westbound coal train at Revelstoke in December 1990 (part of a group of 25 such units delivered in 1988). In the background is Mount Mackenzie, named after the first Liberal Prime Minister of Canada (1873 to 1878), Alexander Mackenzie. *Phil Mason*

With Macdonald out, Liberal leader Alexander Mackenzie became prime minister in November 1873. Though the Liberals had been harsh critics of the Macdonald government's handling of the Pacific railway, they inherited obligations and commitments from which there was no turning back. Surveys to identify a potential route for the railway had been under way since 1871. However, no construction had taken place during the first two years following British Columbia's entry into Canada, and the country was now in an economic depression.

Mackenzie was forced to make at least a modest beginning on the project, and in 1874 he authorized the construction of the first line that would eventually become part of Canadian Pacific. This was not part of the east–west main line, but instead ran south from Winnipeg, Manitoba, to the U.S. border. In conjunction with a rail line south of the border being built at the same time, it would allow construction materials to reach Winnipeg by rail rather than by overland haulage.

Work on the Pembina Branch, as the 63-mile (101-kilometer) line south of Winnipeg was known, proceeded slowly, and the line was not placed into service until 1878. In the meantime, a contract had been signed for construction of a connecting line running 20 miles (32 kilometers) north from Winnipeg, to Selkirk, then eastward to Fort William on Lake Superior. Initial surveys had the east–west transcontinental rail route crossing the Red River at Selkirk, although the route was later changed in favor of Winnipeg.

In the national election of September 1878, Macdonald returned to power and resumed his role as prime minister. Six months earlier, a partnership of four men had acquired control of the St. Paul and Pacific Railroad, which was to be the U.S. connection for the Canadian rail line being built southward from Winnipeg. The partners were James J. Hill, Norman W. Kittson, Donald A.

Smith, and George Stephen. By December 1878, the lines both north and south of the border were completed.

Despite Canada's promise to the citizens of British Columbia in 1871 that they would have their railway within ten years, as the 1870s drew to a close, the government had awarded construction contracts for only 700 miles (1,126 kilometers) of track. These contracts

At Cisco, British Columbia, where Andrew Onderdonk's crews were forced to cross the Fraser River, they erected a steel cantilever bridge, a pioneering work of engineering for its time. After it was replaced in 1909, the cantilever bridge was moved to CPR's Esquimalt & Nanaimo Railway on Vancouver Island. *Samuel J. Jarvis/Library and Archives Canada/ PA-025036*

covered the building of the lines between Lake Superior and Winnipeg, and from Yale to Kamloops Lake, British Columbia.

Economic depression, political turnover, and the lack of able and willing entrepreneurs to take on responsibility for the completion and operation of the railway all led to delays. But with the economy reviving, and Macdonald back in power, two of those handicaps were overcome. The third would soon be rectified as well.

George Stephen, a Scot who had come to Canada in 1850, had served as president of the Bank of Montreal since 1876. He would soon add another presidency to his résumé: that of Canadian Pacific Railway. He was, in Lamb's words, "the heart and soul of the C.P.R. 'syndicate,' as the small closely knit

The original bridge over the Fraser River at Cisco was replaced by this through-truss design in 1909, but the piers and masonry foundations of the first bridge, dating from 1884, were used for the new structure, and remain in service in the twenty-first century. Here, a train of coal empties crosses the bridge in 1985. *Phil Mason*

group that launched the company came to be called, and in its critical first half-dozen years it was in great measure a personal enterprise."

Two other members of the syndicate were, like Stephen, also part of the St. Paul and Pacific group: Stephen's cousin, Donald A. Smith, and James J. Hill. Smith, who came to Canada from Scotland at the age of 18, was a veteran of the Hudson's Bay Company who had risen to be the company's chief commissioner in Canada; he was elected to Parliament in 1871. Hill was born in Ontario but was now a leading businessman in St. Paul, Minnesota; his principal legacy would be the building of the Great Northern Railway from St. Paul to Seattle.

In October 1880, the syndicate agreed to build the 1,900 miles (3,058 kilometers) of track needed to complete the railway (including the challenging segments north of Lake Superior and through the western mountain territory) for $25 million in cash subsidy and a

land grant of 25 million acres (10.1 million hectares). The eastern terminus of the railway would be at Callender, Ontario, near Lake Nipissing. There, it would connect with the Canada Central Railway, which extended from that point to Ottawa.

This contract was for more than construction, however. Stephen and his colleagues agreed to "for ever efficiently maintain, work and run the Canadian Pacific Railway." Following the government's ratification of the contract, the Canadian Pacific Railway Company was incorporated on February 16, 1881.

Overcoming Nature's Barriers

Three major physical challenges faced the surveyors and builders of the railway across Canada:

- The Laurentian Shield, a vast and heavily forested land of rock, muskeg, and rivers north of Lake Superior;

- The Rocky Mountains and other ranges separating the interior of British Columbia from the prairies; and
- The canyons of the Thompson and Fraser rivers, which gave the railway a path to the Pacific but presented numerous engineering challenges.

A key figure in deciding how to overcome these barriers (although some of his advice was later disregarded) was Sandford Fleming. Like many of those involved in the early development of the Pacific railway, Fleming was a Scot. He had served as the chief engineer of the Intercolonial Railway, built to connect Quebec and the Maritime provinces. In 1871, he was selected as the chief engineer of the Pacific railway. Almost immediately upon British Columbia's entry into Canada, his survey parties began their work.

The Fraser and Thompson Rivers

One of Fleming's earliest conclusions was that the most economical route through the Rockies lay through Yellowhead Pass, just west of today's Jasper, Alberta. From that point, the most favorable route to the sea would take the railway down the Upper Thompson River to Kamloops, then via the Thompson and Fraser rivers to the harbor at Burrard Inlet (where Vancouver is now located). Though some pressed for a route that would take the railway to a western terminus farther north, which

This 1881 photo, taken at Tunnel No. 8 between Yale and North Bend, British Columbia, in the Fraser River Canyon, illustrates the physical obstacles that engineer Andrew Onderdonk and his crews had to overcome as they pushed eastward. *Richard Maynard/ Library and Archives Canada/C-07660*

would have allowed for a relatively short ferry trip (or even, some said, a bridge) to Vancouver Island, Fleming's choice of Burrard Inlet was ultimately accepted by the government.

Although only minor progress was made in constructing the railway in the first eight years following British Columbia's entry into Canada, in 1879 the government awarded a contract that showed it was serious about the project. For $9.1 million, American engineer Andrew Onderdonk agreed to construct the 127-mile (204-kilometer) segment between Yale, British Columbia (the point at which the Fraser River became navigable) and Kamloops Lake. The completion date was set for June 30, 1885.

Onderdonk began work at Yale on May 15, 1880. Building a railway up the Fraser Canyon demanded extraordinary amounts of black powder and human muscle. In *The Pictorial History of Railroading in British Columbia*, Barrie Sanford writes that as he began the project, Onderdonk "estimated his manpower requirement at 10,000 men, nearly one-third of the entire provincial

An eastbound train winds along the Thompson River at Thompson, British Columbia, in June 1975. Behind the locomotives is a "robot" car housing remote-control equipment used primarily on westbound tonnage trains. This technology, implemented on CPR beginning in 1967, allowed longer trains to be operated with mid-train power remotely controlled from the lead locomotive. The robot cars were phased out in the 1980s as the equipment became compact enough to be mounted on the locomotives themselves. Remote control is not needed on this eastbound train; the robot car is being transported to a point such as Golden where it will be added to a westbound train. *Steve Patterson*

The original western terminus of the transcontinental railway was Port Moody, British Columbia, on Burrard Inlet. In 1885, CPR reached agreement with the province to extend the line 13 miles (21 kilometers) west to the town of Granville, which was renamed Vancouver. This 1886 photo shows a British man-of-war anchored in the harbor at Port Moody. *Photo by O. B. Buell, courtesy of Glenbow Archives/NA-4140-85*

population at the time." To help meet this need, Onderdonk imported more than 6,000 Chinese laborers.

Onderdonk was forced by his government contract into some shortsighted economies, which required reworking by Canadian Pacific after it took ownership of the Yale–Kamloops Lake segment. However, his success in building the railway through the canyons of the Fraser and the Thompson led to his being awarded two additional construction contracts. One, with the government, covered the 90 miles (145 kilometers) of railway from Yale to Burrard Inlet. The other contract, with Canadian Pacific, was for the 125 miles (201 kilometers) east of Kamloops Lake.

A Crucial Routing Decision: How to Cross the Rockies?

Fleming had recommended a route through Yellowhead Pass, which crossed the Rocky Mountains at the relatively modest elevation of 3,711 feet (1,131 meters). Weighing against this route were several considerations. Yellowhead is roughly 200 miles (321 kilometers) north of the southernmost Canadian mountain passes; keeping the line closer to the international boundary would minimize

Train 2, the eastbound *Canadian*, passes over the 484-foot (148-meter) Stoney Creek Bridge in August 1977. The original wooden bridge, on the east slope of Rogers Pass, was constructed in 1884 and replaced by a steel arch in 1893. That bridge was reinforced in 1929 through the addition of a second arch on each side, in order to accommodate the weight of the 375-ton Selkirk locomotives delivered that year. *Phil Mason*

the risk of U.S. railroads penetrating the border territory. A more southerly line would also have fewer north-south water courses to bridge. Since most of Canada's existing population centers were located within 100 miles (160 kilometers) of the U.S. border, there would also be some savings in rail mileage in comparison with a route that swung north through Yellowhead. Finally, James J. Hill

Canadian West, and whether the change was for better or worse is still a matter of debate." He also observes that the group that made the final decision in favor of a southern crossing of the mountains at a May 1881 meeting in St. Paul—Hill; Stephen; R. B. Angus, a colleague of Stephen's from the Bank of Montreal who was part of the CPR syndicate; and John Macoun, a botanist who had explored the western prairies—left no written record of their specific reasons for doing so. Yellowhead Pass would eventually host the main line of the Grand Trunk Pacific and (briefly) the Canadian Northern Railway, but not until the second decade of the twentieth century.

The syndicate's decision in favor of a southern route left open the question of precisely which passes would be used to traverse the Rockies, the Selkirks, and other mountain ranges of eastern British Columbia. However, even as the syndicate members were meeting in St. Paul, Major A. B. Rogers, a surveying engineer hired by Hill early in 1881, was in the field, seeking a route to connect the prairies and the Pacific.

By the end of the surveying season, Rogers had made a preliminary choice, which would be confirmed by more detailed surveys in 1882 and 1883. The railway would approach the Rockies from the east using the Bow River Valley and cross them at Kicking Horse Pass (elevation 5,332 feet, or 1,625 meters). It would then descend along the Kicking Horse River to what would become the town of Golden. West of that point, the route would cross and then follow the Columbia River and one of its tributaries, the Beaver River, eventually surmounting the Selkirks at a pass located by Rogers in 1882, and subsequently named for him.

Westward from the Selkirks pass, the railway would follow another water course, the Illecillewaet River, to a second crossing of the Columbia, at a point where the town of Revelstoke would be located. The Gold Range (now known as the Monashees) would

believed that a southern route would be preferable because of its proximity to coal deposits in and near southeastern British Columbia.

In the final analysis a crossing of the continental divide at Yellowhead lost out to a southern route. Lamb notes that "It was a momentous decision that altered substantially the future pattern of settlement in the

be surmounted at Eagle Pass. There, CPR would connect with the line to be constructed by Andrew Onderdonk, which would follow relatively easy topography eastward from Kamloops Lake to the Shuswap Highlands, which would be crossed at Notch Hill.

While the work of finding a route through the mountains was proceeding, a new figure entered the CPR story. William Cornelius Van Horne was an American who had risen to the position of general manager on the Chicago, Milwaukee & St. Paul Railroad. At the age of 38, he was recruited by Hill to take a similar position with CPR, and he joined the company on November 1, 1881. He was a renaissance man who devoted himself to learning not just his own job but that of every other person he came into contact with in his career. Because he understood how a railway's engineering, operations, and commercial activ-

The original crossing of Rogers Pass required an elaborate system of loops and wooden trestles to overcome the area's rugged topography. The notes with this 1886 photograph read: "Second crossing of Fivemile Creek, looking north-east. Upper track, right. Sir Donald Range in the background." *Photo by O. B. Buell, courtesy of Glenbow Archives/NA-4140-39*

Nine miles (13 kilometers) west of Lake Louise, and 3 miles (4.5 kilometers) east of the Continental Divide, Train 1, *The Canadian*, passes Wapta Lake at Hector, British Columbia, in June 1975. Hector is named after James Hector, a geologist on the Palliser Expedition of 1857–1860. In 1858, while the Hector party was exploring a tributary of the Columbia River, a horse fell into the river. In the process of retrieving the horse, Hector was kicked and knocked unconscious. The river, and the pass that it led to, came to be known as Kicking Horse. *Steve Patterson*

ities were connected, he was ideally suited to guide CPR through the completion of its east-west rail system. CPR had been a group of bankers and industrialists managing a surveying and construction operation; Van Horne's arrival transformed it into a nascent railway company.

Within a year of Van Horne's arrival, he had recruited former colleague Thomas G. Shaughnessy to join him at CPR. Shaughnessy's title at CM&StP—general storekeeper—belied the range of his abilities. At CPR, he took charge of purchasing. This function was of considerable importance given that the ultimate financial cost of the transcontinental railway was, at its inception, largely a matter of guesswork. Cost control was of the utmost

importance, and Shaughnessy's ability to strike a hard bargain with suppliers helped keep expenses down. Equally important was his ability to keep the supply system running at a smooth and measured pace so that work crews had the right volume of materials at the right time.

During 1882, under Van Horne's leadership, CPR track was pushed westward about 575 miles (925 kilometers) from Winnipeg, and in October trains began operating between Winnipeg and Regina, Saskatchewan, a distance of 350 miles (563 kilometers). The attack on the mountains began the following year. Track crews reached Calgary in August 1883. From that point, says Lamb, "track was *continued on page 30*

continued from page 27

pushed on up the Bow River valley and thence to the Kicking Horse Pass. By November 27, it had neared the summit and there paused for the winter—almost a mile (1.6 kilometers) above sea level and 962 miles (1,548 kilometers) from Winnipeg. The two seasons had witnessed a prodigious construction feat that had never been equaled in railway history."

The pace at which Van Horne had moved west came at some cost, however. The speed of construction (combined with unrealistic cost estimates relied upon by the CPR syndicate when they negotiated their contract with the government) meant that the company was running through its available funds faster than expected. By late 1883, CPR was in financial difficulty, and in early 1884 a $22.5 million loan from the government was arranged to tide the company over. Van Horne was pressured to cut costs wherever he could and to bring the construction project to completion as soon as possible.

One way he responded was to make an exception to the general rule that CPR would be constructed with a ruling gradient of no more than 2.2 percent. West of Kicking Horse Pass, a route had been surveyed that would have complied with that guideline. However, it would have required a tunnel that would not only be expensive for the cash-strapped company, but would also have delayed completion of the line. A more economical descent of the western slope of the Rockies could be built, but it would have a grade of 4.5 percent. This was the route that Van Horne chose to use, and thus was born what became known as CPR's "Big Hill." It was described as a temporary solution, but it would last until the opening of the Spiral Tunnels in 1909.

The line from Kicking Horse Pass to Beavermouth, 22 miles (35 kilometers) east of Rogers Pass, was completed during the 1884 construction season. Rogers Pass, at 4,340 feet (1,322 meters), was almost 1,000 feet (305 meters) lower than Kicking Horse, but presented its own challenges. Several high bridges were required to cross deep gorges in the Beaver River Valley, and more trestles were required west of the summit. On the western slope, heavy snowfall and the threat of avalanches dictated long snowsheds. The severity of this crossing was mitigated by construction of the 5-mile (8-kilometer) Connaught Tunnel, opened in 1916, but in the interim it presented serious operational and maintenance challenges for CPR and its employees.

The Lake Superior Line

At the beginning of 1883, work was nearing completion on the government-built line between Winnipeg and Port Arthur, on Lake Superior, which would be transferred to CPR ownership in May of that year. But only about 40 miles (64 kilometers) of the line between Callender, Ontario, where CPR would connect with the Canada Central, and Port Arthur, had been completed. When Fleming had surveyed this area, he had settled on a route far north of Lake Superior. But George Stephen was determined to put much of the railway along the lake shore. A primary reason was to allow materials to reach the construction zone by water. By late 1883, work was well underway, with 9,500 men

One of the many snowsheds that CPR built in the early years to help keep the line open through the mountains year-round, shown as it was being constructed in the 1880s. CPR spent more than $2 million building snowsheds in 1886 and 1887. *Notman & Son/Library and Archives Canada/C-007674*

employed on construction crews east of Port Arthur. Numerous rock cuts, bridges, and fills were required.

James J. Hill had remained part of the CPR syndicate but by early 1883 he understood that Stephen and Van Horne were committed to building the line north of the lake. Until that time, Hill remained hopeful that the syndicate would come to share his view that an all-Canadian route was foolish, and so he maintained his association with CPR. His St. Paul and Pacific (now the St. Paul, Minneapolis and Manitoba) had profited from hauling construction materials north to the border, but what he really wanted was to see his railway become a link between CPR's eastern and western lines. When he saw that this was not to be, he parted ways with the syndicate.

In May 1884, Van Horne, who had been with CPR for only two-and-one-half years,

The numerous rivers and streams flowing into Lake Superior required extensive use of bridges, such as this one over the Steel River, 14 miles (22 kilometers) east of Schreiber, Ontario. *Library and Archives Canada/C-03411*

was given the title of vice president and made a director of the company. "Thereafter," says Lamb, "the executive committee consisted of George Stephen, Donald Smith, R. B. Angus, and Van Horne—a tightly knit and determined group, sharing the conviction that the company must not and would not fail."

Unlike the route west of Winnipeg, which was pushed forward in a continuous line, the trackage north of Lake Superior was finished in separate segments, dictated by the proximity of supply points and by the time required to bridge major rivers emptying into Lake Superior. During 1884, work progressed at a much more rapid pace than in the prior years, and by the end of that year only a few significant gaps remained. In May 1885, the last segment of this line was completed at Jackfish Bay, Ontario.

A bridge under construction at Nipigon River, Ontario, on the north shore of Lake Superior, 70 miles (113 kilometers) east of Fort William. *Library and Archives Canada/ C-021981*

Near Middleton, Ontario, on the north shore of Lake Superior, in September 1993, Extra 5736 West crosses the Little Pic River Bridge, a curved deck-truss structure that stands 90 feet (27 meters) above the water.
Steve Patterson

The Last Spike

Completion of the line east of Winnipeg left only one gap in the transcontinental route. In personal terms, the gap was between Andrew Onderdonk, whose crews were pushing eastward from Kamloops Lake toward Eagle Pass, and James Ross, CPR's construction superintendent, pushing westward toward the same point from Rogers Pass.

Onderdonk arrived first, in late September, and pronouncing his contract fulfilled, dismissed his crews. Ross did not arrive at the agreed meeting point until November. Given the momentous nature of the event, a ceremony might have been expected. But Van Horne was determined to keep it simple.

The meeting point was named Craigellachie, in honor of a peak in the Spey Valley of Scotland, home to the ancestors of George Stephen and Donald Smith. At 9:22 on the morning of November 7, 1885, Smith drove the last spike; it was made of iron, not precious metal. Van Horne's speech became famous for its brevity and simplicity: "All I can say is that the work has been well done in every way."

In October 1998, SD40-2 CP 5932 leads westbound Train 411 through Jackfish Tunnel on the rugged north shore of Lake Superior. The last spike on the CPR line between Montreal and Winnipeg was driven at Jackfish on May 16, 1885. *John Leopard*

Perhaps the most famous photograph from the early years of Canadian Pacific, this scene depicts the last-spike ceremony at Craigellachie, British Columbia, on November 7, 1885. The key figures shown are Donald Smith (driving the spike), Sandford Fleming (top hat, behind Smith), and William Cornelius Van Horne (to Fleming's right). The line through the mountains would soon be closed for the winter, reopening in the spring of 1886. *Alexander Ross/Library and Archives Canada/C-003693*

At Chokio, between Fort Macleod and Brocket, Alberta, CP 5712 is eastbound on the Crowsnest Subdivision, constructed in 1897 and 1898. The Livingston Range of the Rockies is in the distance. *John Leopard*

CHAPTER TWO

BECOMING A GLOBAL TRANSPORTATION SYSTEM: *1885–1918*

In the decade following the opening of the transcontinental main line,

CPR's owners were faced with a dilemma. The enterprise was, as John

Lorne McDougall observed, "desperately premature." In the near term,

there were no sources of traffic along the newly developed lines.

To complicate matters, the railway was essentially a seasonal

enterprise west of Calgary. During the long winter, heavy snowfall and

avalanches kept the line closed for extended periods. To keep the line

open, more men and equipment had to be employed during winter

Six 0-6-6-0 Mallet locomotives were delivered between 1909 and 1912 for pusher service out of Field, British Columbia, but they were hard to maintain. In 1916 and 1917 they were rebuilt as 2-10-0 Decapods. CPR Class R2B 2-10-0 5752, at Montreal in August 1956, was one of these locomotives. *Jim Shaughnessy*

than in the summer. But revenues fell during the winter, creating pressure on the company's treasury to maintain the cash flow to pay employees and suppliers.

CPR could not stand still and wait for business to develop. It had to grow its network in order to become economically self-sustaining. Between 1885 and 1896, it expanded its route miles from 3,998 (6,434 kilometers) to 6,476 (10,422), an increase of 62 percent. Much of this growth came in the East, where, unlike the area from Lake Superior west, there was a developed economy and an established need for rail service.

Truly Transcontinental:
CPR Reaches the Atlantic

Even as CPR was pushing westward, it had been extending its reach in the East. Part of George Stephen's vision for the company was that it would be the critical middle sec-tion of a water-land-water route between Britain and Asia. To fulfill that role, it needed good access to a year-round port. Montreal, closed to shipping for much of the winter, did not meet that need.

The most ready access to Atlantic ports was via railroads already in operation in New England. In 1883, CPR acquired the South Eastern Railway, which extended through Quebec to Newport, Vermont. There, it connected with the Passumpsic Railroad, which acted as a bridge to other New England railroads serving the ports of Boston and Portland.

A trio of 1958-vintage Montreal Locomotives Works (MLW) RS-18 units is in charge of CPR Train 904 at McIndoes, Vermont, in February 1973. In another 8 miles (13 kilometers) the train will reach the interchange point with the Boston & Maine at Wells River, Vermont, but the crew will take the train another 40 miles (65 kilometers) beyond Wells River to the B&M yard at White River Junction. At right is the Connecticut River. *Tom Murray*

In the same year, CPR gained control of the Atlantic and North-West Railway, which had been chartered to build between the Atlantic Coast and Lake Superior, to construct a bridge over the St. Lawrence River near Montreal, and to build a line across northern Maine between Quebec and New Brunswick. This international route to the Maritimes was known as the Short Line. With this route in hand, CPR would be able to connect from Saint John, New Brunswick, to Halifax, Nova Scotia, via the Intercolonial Railway. In 1889, the first CPR train reached Saint John. The relationship with the Intercolonial would prove frustrating and unworkable for CPR, but the company had at least established a beachhead in the Atlantic provinces.

CPR's growth in the East was not limited to a route from Montreal to the Atlantic. In 1887, it opened a new line from Montreal to

Smiths Falls, Ontario, thereby improving its Montreal–Toronto route. Three years later, it reached Windsor, where it was able to connect (via ferry) with the Wabash Railway in Michigan. With this route in operation, CPR had completed its basic network in southern Ontario.

Both CPR and Grand Trunk had their eye on Sault Ste. Marie as a way of connecting with U.S. railways that were building toward that point from the west. GT, which deeply resented CPR's aggressive push into southern Ontario, tried to forestall CPR from reaching the Sault gateway by acquiring various lines that gave it a toehold in the region northwest of Toronto. But CPR had a strategic advantage because it had already reached from Montreal to Sudbury, Ontario, where a line to the Sault would connect with its transcontinental main line. GT claimed that

Above: The line between Mattawamkeag and Vanceboro, Maine, was built by the European and North American Railway in 1871 as part of a route from Bangor to Saint John, New Brunswick, and operated by the Maine Central Railroad (with CPR holding trackage rights beginning in 1889). Here, Train 981 from Saint John to Montreal passes the station at Mattawamkeag, leaving Maine Central rails for CPR's, in October 1970. The track in the foreground is Maine Central's route to Bangor. The Mattawamkeag–Vanceboro line was purchased by CPR in 1974. *Tom Murray* **Below:** An eastbound intermodal train from Chicago to Montreal passes Newtonville, Ontario, in October 1986, with CPR and Soo Line power. In the foreground is Canadian National's Montreal–Toronto main line. *Eric Blasko*

Completion of CPR's route between Montreal, Quebec, and Windsor, Ontario, in the late 1880s made CPR a head-to-head competitor with rival Grand Trunk. Detroit–Toronto Train 516 is at Milton, Ontario, in July 1993, having just descended Campbellville Hill and the Niagara Escarpment (seen in the background). CP 4713, an MLW M-636, leads the train. *John Leopard*

it held a charter to build to the Sault, but CPR moved forward anyway, reaching Sault Ste. Marie in 1888.

CPR intended to connect at Sault Ste. Marie with the Duluth, South Shore & Atlantic Railway and with the Minneapolis, St. Paul & Sault Ste. Marie Railway. The former would give CPR access to Duluth, the latter to St. Paul and Minneapolis. CPR lacked the capital to buy these railroads, but George Stephen and Donald Smith stepped into the breach and, using their own funds, gained control of both companies in 1888.

The following year, through train service was established between Boston and St. Paul by way of Montreal and the Sault. That same year, CPR helped both companies avoid bankruptcy. In return for CPR's guarantee of their bonds they entered into "secure and permanent" traffic arrangements with CPR.

W. Kaye Lamb summarizes the nine-year period beginning with the formation of the company in 1881:

> By 1890 the Canadian Pacific's entire eastern network was approaching completion.

CP 5007 was one of 12 2,500-horsepower GP35 units acquired in 1964. Here, it leads an MLW FB2 and FA2 upgrade at Campbellville, Ontario, on the Niagara Escarpment. *Bill Linley*

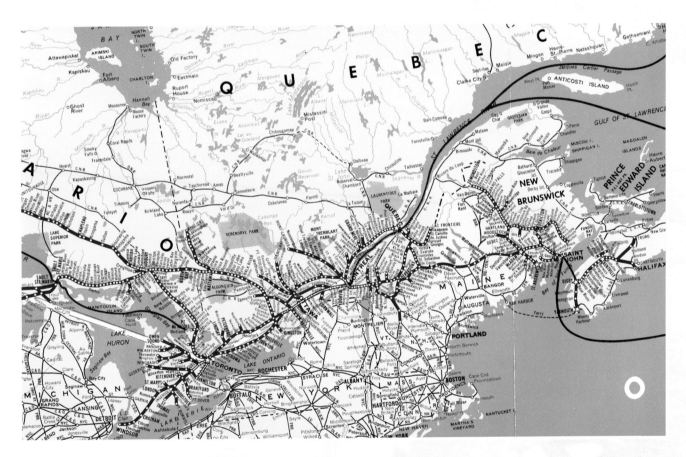

Excerpt from a 1957 map showing CPR rail lines in eastern Ontario, Quebec, the Maritime Provinces, and New England. Today, the CPR network goes as far east as Montreal, with lines east of that point having been sold, leased, or abandoned. However, as a result of the 1991 acquisition of Delaware & Hudson Railway and other U.S. transactions, CPR now serves Binghamton and Albany, New York, and Harrisburg, Pennsylvania, and reaches New York City, Philadelphia, and Washington, D.C., via trackage, haulage, or marketing rights. *Author collection*

This bridge, on the Kicking Horse River in British Columbia, shows the heavy use that CPR's builders made of the material most readily available to them: wood. By doing so, they completed the line as quickly as possible, but the railway had to replace many wooden structures within the first decade after the transcontinental route was completed in 1885. This photo was taken circa 1887–1889. *Photo by Boorne and May, courtesy of Glenbow Archives/NA-1753-6*

Extending from Saint John, Quebec, Montreal, and Ottawa to Toronto, Windsor, and Detroit, and from Sault Ste. Marie over affiliated lines to Duluth and St. Paul, it exceeded considerably in span the system of its great rival, the Grand Trunk. To have built the main line to the Pacific and acquired this network in only nine years was indeed a remarkable accomplishment.

Rebuilding the Railway

The completion of the transcontinental line in 1885 was more of a beginning than an end. "Low first cost" had been the guiding princi-

ple of the railway's builders, and while William Van Horne had ensured that the line would be safe to operate, it was neither efficient nor economical. As Lamb describes the physical condition of the CPR in 1885:

For hundreds of miles it consisted of little more than the ties and the two rails that rested upon them, with a row of telegraph poles along one side carrying two wires on a single stubby crosstree . . . it was a characteristic of pioneer railways that, having been built, they must forthwith be rebuilt, and much of the main line of the Canadian

Pacific was no exception. Solvent, but nonetheless chronically short of money, the C.P.R. had to begin this task immediately after its nominal completion.

The needs included equipment, loading platforms, warehouses, ballast, straightening of curves, widening of cuts, reduction of grades, and improvement of bridges and culverts.

Given the company's limited funds, and the emphasis on extending itself eastward, the serious task of rebuilding did not actually begin until 1890. One of the most visible—and critical—improvements was replacement of the hastily built timber structures that dotted the CPR from one end of Canada to the other. Between 1890 and 1895, the company would replace 2,178 wooden bridges with steel, masonry arches, fill, thus allowing for the operation of heavier equipment while at the same time eliminating a fire hazard. In addition, 72-pound rails replaced the 56-pound rails used during construction, and many grades and curves were reduced.

The rebuilding of Canadian Pacific has continued right up to the present day, with the improvement of engineering and construction techniques, the growth of traffic, and the evolution of operating strategies.

Meeting the American Challenge in Southern British Columbia

George Stephen (later Lord Mount Stephen) resigned as president of CPR in 1888. He remained as a director of the company, and Van Horne moved into the presidency. One of the major challenges that Van Horne faced during his entire time in this position was the struggle for rail dominance in the Kootenay and Okanagan regions of southern British Columbia. Ironically, his foe in this struggle was a man who had been present at the creation of Canadian Pacific and had, in fact, recommended Van Horne for his first post at CPR: James J. Hill.

Although Hill and Stephen worked together to advance each other's ventures, by the time Stephen resigned as president of CPR, their diverging interests had complicated the relationship. Hill resented the fact that Stephen, along with Donald Smith, had gained control of the two U.S. railroads running westward from Sault Ste. Marie. One of Stephen's last acts as president was to arrange for CPR to purchase these properties (from himself and Smith).

Stephen and Hill continued to collaborate in the 1890s, particularly on Hill's takeover of the Northern Pacific, but Van Horne had come to view Hill as an adversary

Nelson, British Columbia, was the largest terminal on the Crowsnest Pass–Kettle Valley route through southern British Columbia. CP 5758, next to the coaling tower, is a Class R3b 2-10-0, built in 1917 at CPR's Angus Shops in Montreal. This photo is from May 1951. *Photo by Philip Hastings, courtesy of California State Railroad Museum/ negative no. 200*

who could not be trusted, and whose business interests would invariably be contrary to those of the Canadian Pacific.

Van Horne's view was confirmed by the outcome of a battle with Hill for control of a small railroad in Minnesota. In 1892, CPR, through the Duluth, South Shore & Atlantic, gained control of the Duluth & Winnipeg Railway, running northwest from Duluth. Van Horne saw this as a key link in a CPR route from Duluth to the West. But Hill wanted it for himself, and quietly bought up the railway's

debt. In 1897, Hill took control of the D&W, which would become Great Northern's route into the Minnesota Iron Range.

By the early 1890s, deposits of gold, silver, zinc, and copper had been discovered in the Kootenay area of southern British Columbia. Since the Columbia River flowed south into the United States, Washington State stood to benefit more than British Columbia from the smelting and other activities it would take to develop these resources, unless Canadians took steps to prevent this.

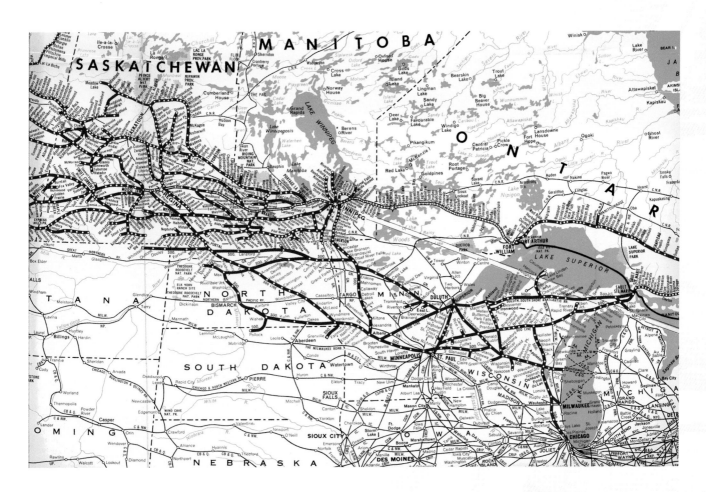

Excerpt from a 1957 map showing CPR rail lines in Saskatchewan, Manitoba, and western Ontario. The company's U.S. affiliate, Soo Line Railroad, served the upper midwestern states. Today, many Soo Line routes in Wisconsin and Michigan are part of Canadian National, and CPR's St. Paul–Chicago route consists of trackage formerly operated by the Milwaukee Road. As a result of Soo Line's 1985 acquisition of the Milwaukee Road, CPR also reached into Indiana and as far south as Louisville, Kentucky, via trackage rights. In 2005, CPR said it would sell the Louisville line to a regional carrier, Indiana Rail Road. After many years of holding a majority interest in Soo Line, CPR gained full control of the U.S. road in 1990 and has since integrated it into the CPR system. *Author collection*

Hill made no secret of his intention to reach the Kootenay region via branch lines from his Great Northern Railway. In 1892, Van Horne, seeking to establish a CPR presence in the Kootenay before Hill, opened a 28-mile (45-kilometer) line between Nelson and Robson, connecting Kootenay Lake with the Columbia River. Soon, CPR had steamer service operating on the Columbia River between Revelstoke and Robson.

The next year, the first American railway arrived in southern British Columbia, reaching the outskirts of Nelson from Spokane, Washington. It was the creation not of Hill,

but of another entrepreneur, D. C. Corbin. However, it was equally suspect from Van Horne's perspective, especially since it connected with the Great Northern at Spokane.

Development of the region's mining industry took a major step forward with the opening of a smelter at Trail Creek, next to the Columbia River, in 1896. The smelter operator built a line along the river northward to Robson and talked about plans to go farther. In 1898, CPR gained control of the railway and with it, the smelter. With this acquisition, the company found itself in the metal-refining business. The smelter at Trail

A set of five Canadian Locomotive Company (CLC) H16-44 units eases down the 3.61 percent grade of Poupore Hill, British Columbia, en route to the CPR yard at Tadanac, in October 1972. This line, along the Columbia River north of Trail, was originally constructed in 1897 by Augustus Heinze, who opened the first smelter at Trail. *Tom Murray*

Creek was the beginning of an important Canadian Pacific subsidiary, Consolidated Mining and Smelting, which would later be known as Cominco.

The ore that fed the Trail Creek smelter came from Rossland, 13 miles (21 kilometers) distant. Corbin built a second rail line into southern British Columbia, this one extending to Rossland from Northport, Washington. In 1898, this line passed into the control of Hill.

Van Horne knew that in order to be a meaningful participant in the growing economy of southern British Columbia, CPR

needed an east–west line through the region, connecting with Lethbridge in the East and Vancouver in the West. But the cost of constructing a line into the Kootenay from the east exceeded CPR's financial resources. Starting in the early 1890s, CPR made various proposals for the government to subsidize this route.

These efforts came to fruition in 1897 with a pact between the company and the government of Canada, known as the Crow's Nest Pass Agreement, that was given effect by an Act of Parliament on June 29, 1897. A subsidy of $11,000 per mile would be granted to CPR, in return for which the railway would grant rate concessions on certain commodities moving to and from the Prairie provinces. It must have seemed like a sensible arrangement to the parties involved, but CPR's agreement to make permanent rate

Above: The S.S. *Rossland* was launched in 1897 as part of CPR's steamboat operations in the Kootenays. British Columbia historian Robert D. Turner has described it as "the fastest steamer on the Upper Columbia and a beautifully-proportioned vessel as well." In this 1911 photo, the *Rossland* is shown on Arrow Lake. *Canada Patent and Copyright Office/Library and Archives Canada/C-021044*

Below: Excerpt from a 1957 map showing CPR rail lines in British Columbia and Alberta. The Spokane International, running 149 miles (240 kilometers) from Eastgate, Idaho, to Spokane, was sold to Union Pacific in February 1958, but has remained an important conduit for CPR traffic destined to the western United States. The white line across the southern part of the two provinces represents Canadian Pacific Airlines' transcontinental route. *Author collection*

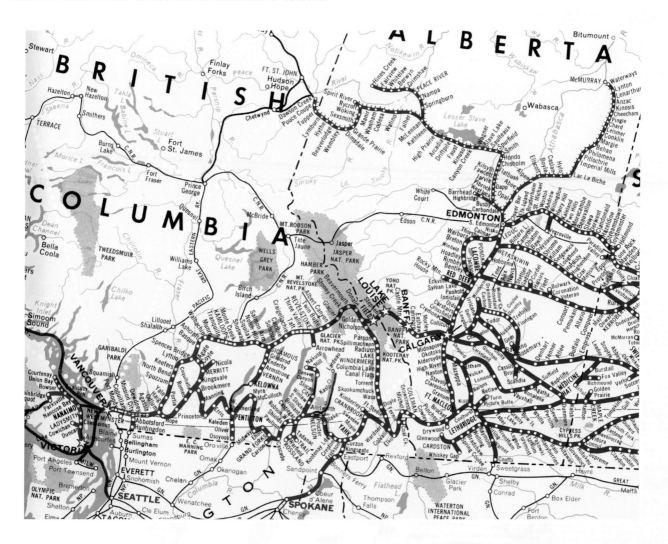

The Tadanac Yard crew waits in the clear while the crew on the freight from Nelson, British Columbia, behind CLC C-Liner 4105, yards its train in October 1972. The industrial facility behind CLC Train Master (Model H24-66) 8905 is part of Cominco's Trail, British Columbia, lead and zinc smelter complex. Cominco, originally the Consolidated Mining and Smelting Company of Canada, was controlled by Canadian Pacific from 1906 to 1986. *Tom Murray*

reductions on grain moving to Fort William and Port Arthur would become an enduring source of controversy for decades.

As it moved westward toward the Kootenay region, the Crowsnest line reached an area of southeastern British Columbia rich in coal deposits. The coal traffic generated here helped feed the energy-hungry smelter operations in the Kootenay. Longer term, coal traffic became a mainstay of CPR's western business, particularly after Canadian coal companies developed export markets in the 1970s, and Canadian Pacific itself became a major player in the region's coal business.

The objective of the Crowsnest line was Nelson, British Columbia, the eastern gateway to the Kootenay mining region, but CPR would not reach that objective for more than 30 years. When operations over the Crowsnest line began in 1898, the western terminus at Kootenay Landing was 55 miles (88 kilometers) short of Nelson, with steamer, tug, and barge service connecting the two points. Four years later the line was extended 20 miles (32 kilo-

meters) to Proctor, and finally, in 1930, construction was completed on the difficult segment along Kootenay Lake between Proctor and Nelson.

While the Crowsnest line approached the Kootenay from the East, CPR was also at work on a line westward toward the coast. It began with a line approximately 100 miles (161 kilometers) in length from Robson west to Grand Forks and Midway, which was completed in 1899.

Although CPR control of the smelter at Trail Creek (now known simply as Trail) had frustrated Hill's ambitions in that area, farther west he was more successful. He gained control of the Granby Company, owner of three major smelters in the Grand Forks area, and, via a Great Northern branch, controlled much of their rail traffic.

Even though Great Northern was an annoyance in southern British Columbia, *continued on page 56*

In May 1951, a pair of 2-8-0 Consolidations, CP 3676 and CP 3626, power a northbound freight leaving the Tadanac Yard near Trail, British Columbia. The bridge crosses Topping Creek, a tributary of the Columbia River. *Photo by Philip Hastings, courtesy of California State Railroad Museum/negative no. 2523*

Above: CP 4065, a Fairbanks-Morse-designed, CLC-built model CPA16-4, began life as a CLC demonstrator and was purchased by CPR in 1951. Here, it leads the westbound Michel switcher at Elko, British Columbia, in September 1972. This unit has been preserved for possible restoration. *Stan Smaill* **Opposite:** CP 8723, a CLC H16-44, leads the Tadanac freight across the Topping Creek Bridge and prepares to enter the Tadanac Yard in October 1972. A sure-footed head brakeman prepares to dismount and line the switch into the yard. *Tom Murray*

In the early 1970s, the diesel shop at Nelson, British Columbia, was home to CPR's remaining fleet of Fairbanks-Morse-designed, CLC-built diesels, including both road switchers and a handful of C-Liner cab units like CP 4105. On this day in October 1972, the 4105 leads the Nelson–Tadanac turn, en route back to Nelson, just north of Trail. *Tom Murray*

Above: At Slocan City, British Columbia, in 1975, the CPR barge is loaded for the 20-mile (32-kilometer) trip across Slocan Lake to Roseberry on the isolated Kaslo Subdivision. Once the cars and engine (GP9 8637) are loaded onto the barge, it will be propelled across the lake by the tugboat. *Iris G. Steve Patterson* **Opposite:** Barge service was provided on Lake Slocan in southern British Columbia from 1897 to 1988. In August 1977, when this photo was taken, CPR provided once-weekly barge service from Slocan City (shown here) at the end of a branch off the Boundary Subdivision. *Phil Mason*

An all-General Motors consist of three GP9s and an F7B lead Train 53 west across the Kettle River Bridge at milepost 81.5 on the Boundary Subdivision, Cascade, British Columbia. Train 53 was a daily freight from Nelson to Midway. This line was abandoned in 1990. *Phil Mason*

continued from page 51
CPR continued to push westward toward its objective of a link with the main line to Vancouver. A CPR-financed company, the Kettle Valley Railway, completed the last segments in this route. As Lamb notes, "The construction, over difficult and often treacherous terrain, was a daunting task of engineering and perseverance, especially through the Coquihalla Pass, which Sandford Fleming had rejected as a possible route for the CPR main line because of narrowness, heavy snowfall and avalanches." The line required many bridges, snowsheds, and tunnels. It was opened to a connection with the main line at Hope in July 1916, "and its completion provided the CPR with another east–west route through British Columbia."

Exit Van Horne

The building, rebuilding, and expansion of Canadian Pacific during the period 1881 to 1899 represented the combined effort of thousands of individuals, but the three who played the most visible roles were its first three presidents: George Stephen, the financier and visionary; William Cornelius Van Horne, the railroader and taskmaster; and Thomas George Shaughnessy, the detail-oriented administrator.

The three complemented each other well during the construction and early operation of the railway. Once the company's foundation was in place, Stephen moved into the background, allowing Van Horne's skills as a railroad operating man, salesman, leader, and motivator to come to the fore. But as the 1890s drew to a close, the challenges of running CPR grew somewhat less daunting, and overcoming them less exciting to Van Horne. In 1899 he resigned from the presidency but stayed on as chairman. He was no longer a powerful voice in the affairs of Canadian Pacific, although even in retirement many outsiders still looked at him as the personification of the the company.

Van Horne's importance to the company was summarized by the Canadian Railway Hall of Fame:

Incredibly, while the CPR's contract with the government dictated completion of the road within a decade, Van Horne—through sheer determination—found ways to finish it in five. Even more remarkably, once Van Horne had completed the CPR, he operated it and, despite the economic malaise for most of the 1880s and 1890s, made it into a paying proposition. Surely, the Canadian Pacific's role as an instrument of Canadian nationalism would have followed a different course, had Van Horne not been at the helm.

Shaughnessy was officially in charge of purchasing for the company during its construction, but his role might today be described as "chief logistics officer." He was responsible for seeing not only that good deals were struck with the company's suppliers but that there was an efficient flow of men and materials toward the front lines as the railroad built west. His skills at managing the company's cash flow—stretching out the payment of bills to creditors,

The year is 1905, and a passenger train arrives at Innisfail, Alberta, on CPR's Calgary–Edmonton line. The water tank is of typical CPR design, with the ball at the top indicating the water level. *Glenbow Archives/NA-1709-71*

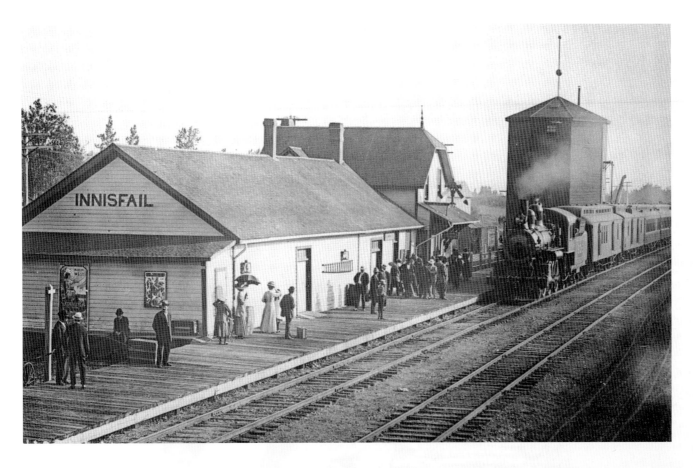

Class P1b 2-8-2 No. 5068 powers a westbound CPR passenger train near Leanchoil, British Columbia. The date of the photo is believed to be between 1913 and 1920. *Andrew Merrilees/Library and Archives Canada/PA-143158*

while insisting on timely payment of sums owed to CPR—helped the company weather the financial crises that plagued it during the years of construction and early operation.

As Van Horne became preoccupied with the Duluth & Winnipeg affair, Shaughnessy

teen years as CPR president, from 1899 to 1918, were as full of fortune as Van Horne's and George Stephen's were dogged by misfortune. It seemed as if all the gods of railway prosperity were cooperating. The company's profitability was staggering."

CPR Extends Its Presence in the United States

CPR had reached into the upper midwestern states through the 1888 acquisition of the Minneapolis, St. Paul & Sault Ste. Marie (commonly known as the Soo Line) and the Duluth, South Shore & Atlantic, both of which connected with CPR at Sault Ste. Marie. In 1893, a second link was established with the Soo Line when it built a line across North Dakota to a location in the northwestern corner of the state, which was given an appropriate name for an international rail gateway: Portal. CPR built a branch from Moose Jaw, Saskatchewan, to complete the link; the station on the Canadian side of the border was called North Portal.

During the Shaughnessy years CPR's U.S. presence was enhanced in various ways. CPR's Pembina branch, south of Winnipeg, connected with Great Northern, but GN was no longer a friendly connection. To rectify that, Soo Line built a line of its own from Glenwood, Minnesota (on the Minneapolis–Portal line), to Noyes, Minnesota, across the border from the CPR station of Emerson, Manitoba. The line was completed in 1904. Soo Line now connected with CPR at three points on the international boundary.

In 1909, Soo Line leased the Wisconsin Central, a railroad that connected the Twin Cities of Minneapolis and St. Paul with Chicago. It also had a network of lines in Wisconsin that reached as far north as the Twin Ports of Duluth and Superior, and to Ashland, Wisconsin. This gave CPR control of a continuous line of railroad extending all the way from western Canada to Chicago.

effectively became the chief operating officer of Canadian Pacific. Upon Van Horne's resignation, he received the title of president.

As David Cruise and Alison Griffiths describe it in their book, *Lords of the Line: The Men Who Built the CPR*, "Shaughnessy's nine-

continued on page 62

Top: At Portal, North Dakota, a Soo Line crew from Harvey, North Dakota, has arrived with a train for the CPR. The CP crew will tie their caboose onto the rear of the westbound train before departing for Moose Jaw, Saskatchewan. *Phil Mason* **Above:** A set of 1949-built General Motors (Electro-Motive Division) F7 units powers Soo Line Train 86 as it departs Thief River Falls, Minnesota, headed for Minneapolis, in April 1974. On the head end are several cars of grain and pulpwood from local Soo Line origins, but most of the train consists of potash, liquefied petroleum gas, and forest products from CPR origins, interchanged to Soo at the Emerson, Manitoba/Noyes, Minnesota border crossing. *Tom Murray* **Opposite:** The rear of Extra CP 5856 West passes over the head end of the train, which is exiting the lower portal of the Upper Spiral Tunnel in June 1978. *Phil Mason*

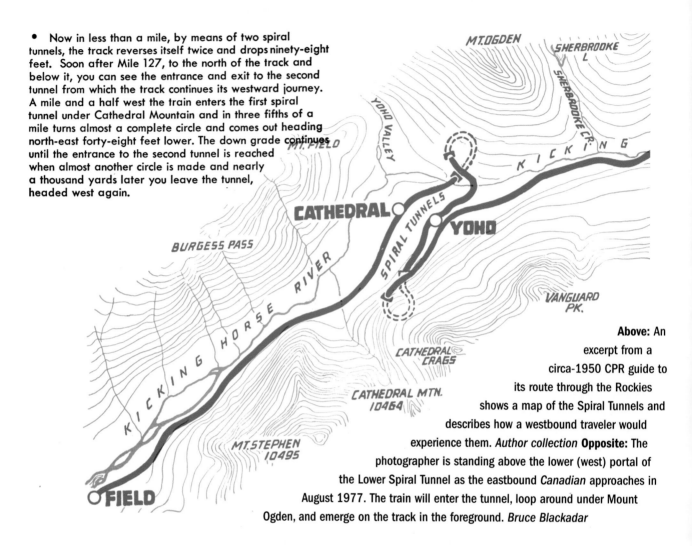

• Now in less than a mile, by means of two spiral tunnels, the track reverses itself twice and drops ninety-eight feet. Soon after Mile 127, to the north of the track and below it, you can see the entrance and exit to the second tunnel from which the track continues its westward journey. A mile and a half west the train enters the first spiral tunnel under Cathedral Mountain and in three fifths of a mile turns almost a complete circle and comes out heading north-east forty-eight feet lower. The down grade continues until the entrance to the second tunnel is reached when almost another circle is made and nearly a thousand yards later you leave the tunnel, headed west again.

Above: An excerpt from a circa-1950 CPR guide to its route through the Rockies shows a map of the Spiral Tunnels and describes how a westbound traveler would experience them. *Author collection* **Opposite:** The photographer is standing above the lower (west) portal of the Lower Spiral Tunnel as the eastbound *Canadian* approaches in August 1977. The train will enter the tunnel, loop around under Mount Ogden, and emerge on the track in the foreground. *Bruce Blackadar*

continued from page 59

CPR also extended its reach into Great Northern's backyard in Washington State. In 1906, D. C. Corbin completed the Spokane International Railway from Spokane to Eastport, Idaho (across the border from Kingsgate, British Columbia). There, it connected with a CPR branch line that in turn connected with the Crowsnest Pass route. In 1917, CPR purchased the Spokane International.

Taming the Passes: Kicking Horse and Rogers

Shaughnessy would leave his mark in many ways, but key physical improvements were among the most important and most lasting. One of the major operating obstacles that limited CPR's operations west of Calgary was the Big Hill between Laggan (Lake Louise) and Field, British Columbia. Surveys aimed at improving the route through Kicking Horse Pass, and eliminating the 4.5 percent descending grade westward into Field, began in 1902.

Although various solutions were considered, the one that was finally chosen was a pair of spiral tunnels that would provide for a substantial change in elevation in the smallest possible area, reducing the eastward ruling grade to 2.2 percent.

As George Buck describes the tunnels in his history of railways in British Columbia and Alberta, *From Summit To Sea*, "the upper, or Number One, encountered first approaching from the east, would curve through 234° in 3,255 feet, and would drop the line by forty-eight feet. The lower—Number Two—

Above: The head end of CPR Extra 5592 East has emerged from the Lower Spiral Tunnel and is about to cross the Kicking Horse River as it makes the ascent through Yoho toward the Upper Spiral Tunnel.
Steve Patterson

Right: An SD40-2 /SD40 consist leads a westbound train exiting the Connaught Tunnel in June 1973.
Phil Mason

curved 232° in 2,921 feet, and would drop the line by forty-five feet to the valley of the Kicking Horse River." The tunnels opened in August 1909.

In Rogers Pass, avalanches had been a continuing problem, particularly in 1899 and again in 1910, when 62 people were killed by slides. In 1912, Shaughnessy announced a program to double-track the crossing of Rogers Pass, using a tunnel that would be 5 miles (8 kilometers) long and reduce the westbound grade to less than 1 percent.

The bore was placed into service in December 1916 and named the Connaught Tunnel in honor of the governor-general of Canada. The new line built to reach the tunnel extended from near Stoney Creek in the East to Ross Peak in the West.

Competition from Canadian Northern and Grand Trunk

In the first decade of the twentieth century, two separate plans were developed for new transcontinental railways. One was the brainchild of William Mackenzie and Donald Mann, whose Canadian Northern Railway (CNoR) was getting more than a toehold in the prairies where CPR had previously enjoyed a monopoly. They were determined to extend their railway from its Manitoba base both eastward and westward; by 1915 CNoR would connect Montreal and Vancouver.

CPR's eastern rival, Grand Trunk, was also in an expansionist frame of mind. Under the leadership of Charles M. Hays, who became the railway's general manager in 1896, a two-part plan was developed. It would extend Grand Trunk's reach from Moncton, New Brunswick, in the East to Prince Rupert, British Columbia, in the West. East of Winnipeg, a federally financed and constructed railway, the National Transcontinental, would be leased to Grand Trunk upon completion. GT would operate it as part of a through route connecting with the GT-built Grand Trunk Pacific, to be built from Winnipeg to Prince Rupert.

Both projects were born of a giddy optimism that could see no end to the country's economic expansion. Both would be undone

This 1915 profile shows the CPR route between Calgary in the east and Kamloops, British Columbia, in the west. At Rogers Pass, it gives both the original elevation (4,340 feet, or 1,323 meters) and the height of the line then being built, which would use the Connaught Tunnel (3,801 feet, or 939 meters). Author collection

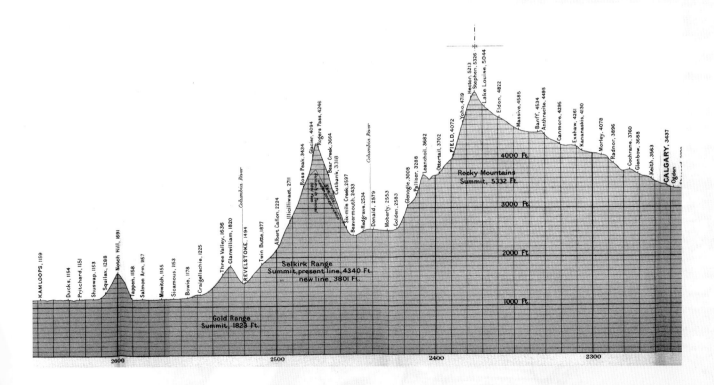

Class D10j 4-6-0 970, built by MLW in 1912, awaits the morning call on a cold night at Sutton, Quebec, in December 1955. *Jim Shaughnessy*

by economic decline and the coming of World War I.

CNoR was financed largely by debt and by cash subsidies for construction. This fragile plan quickly came undone as CNoR faced the dual challenge of building through mountainous territory to reach the Pacific and a slackening of immigration to the prairies, which had helped put traffic onto its network of main and branch lines. Mackenzie and Mann secured financial help from the government, but at the cost of surrendering much of their stock in the closely held company.

GTP's problems were somewhat different in origin but similar in results. Its lines west of Winnipeg were built to a high standard, and it had relatively few branch lines to feed traffic onto the main line. It was also obligated to lease the National Transcontinental when that line was completed across the

The 4-6-0 type was a popular and long-lived engine on CPR. This example, a Class D4g engine built at CPR's Angus Shops in 1915, was, according to photographer Shaughnessy, "the last D-4 class Ten-Wheeler in the Kingston, Ontario, engine house" when this photo was taken in July 1956. *Jim Shaughnessy*

EFFECTIVE JUNE 30 1913

DOMINION
ATLANTIC
RAILWAY

LAND OF EVANGELINE ROUTE

BETWEEN HALIFAX, N.S. & St. JOHN, N.B.,
VIA
DOMINION ATLANTIC RAILWAY
STEAMSHIP LINE
TO AND FROM DIGBY, N.S.,
CONNECTING AT St. JOHN, N.B.,
WITH TRAINS OF THE
CANADIAN PACIFIC RAILWAY

EFFECTIVE JUNE 30 1913

DOMINION
ATLANTIC
RAILWAY

LAND OF EVANGELINE ROUTE

BETWEEN BOSTON, HALIFAX, N.S.,
AND OTHER
MARITIME PROVINCE POINTS
VIA YARMOUTH, N.S.,
THERE CONNECTING WITH STEAMSHIPS
OF THE
BOSTON AND YARMOUTH
STEAMSHIP CO., LIMITED
YARMOUTH
• LINE •

In 1910, CPR obtained control of the Dominion Atlantic Railway in Nova Scotia, which extended CPR's route map eastward to Halifax. The DAR connected with the CPR through a steamer service across the Bay of Fundy, between Saint John, New Brunswick, and Digby, Nova Scotia. The cover of this 1913 Dominion Atlantic timetable advertises not only the Bay of Fundy service but also the steamer services available between Yarmouth, Nova Scotia, and Boston. *Author collection*

wilderness region between Winnipeg and eastern Canada, but construction costs had been higher than expected (and rental fees would follow suit). It, too, sought help from Ottawa, which was given at the cost of a first mortgage on the property. GTP's parent company, Grand Trunk, increased its own exposure through cash advances to the subsidiary.

CPR's view was that the financial difficulties of these companies should be worked out through bankruptcy proceedings, but with a war under way, the government was unwilling to take any chances. It continued to prop up the two railways and thus started down the road toward nationalization.

Seeing that nationalization was all but inevitable, Shaughnessy proposed that CPR itself be part of the scheme by becoming manager of a combined enterprise—CPR, CNoR, and GTP—free of government involvement. But important constituencies, particularly on the prairies, resisted any return to the monopoly that CPR had once enjoyed and (in their view) abused.

Shaughnessy proposed an alternative plan: CPR would buy CNoR, leaving the

Folder A

MARCH 7th, 1905

Visit Banff in the Winter.
Sanitarium Hotel Open for Guests

CANADIAN
PACIFIC
RAILWAY

C. E. McPHERSON,
General Passenger Agent,
Western Lines,
WINNIPEG, MAN.

C. E. E. USSHER,
General Passenger Agent,
Eastern Lines,
MONTREAL.

ROBERT KERR,
Passenger Traffic Manager,
MONTREAL.

The cover of a March 1905 CPR timetable shows the company's view of its potential market: the entire globe, or at least the northern hemisphere. *Author collection*

well-constructed GTP as a competitor. However, this plan, too, was rejected. CPR was left with the specter of a rival rail system with access to the federal treasury and none of the do-or-die imperatives of private enterprise to guide its investing and ratemaking policies.

Between 1917 and 1923, CNoR, GTP, and Grand Trunk were folded in stages into a national enterprise to be known as Canadian National Railways. CNoR was the first to be nationalized, becoming part of a government system that already included the Intercolonial Railway in the Maritime Provinces, as well as the government-built National Transcontinental. GTP followed in 1919, and after considerable legal wrangling, Grand Trunk was forced into the system in January 1923.

Canadian Pacific's Navy

The builders of the CPR, and George Stephen in particular, had conceived the railway "as part of an all-British through route from Europe to the Orient." In late 1885, CPR offered to provide a mail service between Great Britain and the Far East via transatlantic steamer, railway, and transpacific steamer. Nothing came of this offer at the time, but it signaled the company's intention to make the railway the centerpiece of a global transportation enterprise. CPR was more successful two years later when it again offered to provide such a service; this time, its bid was accepted.

CPR's contract to provide the international mail service between Britain and Asia was signed in mid-1889, and three months later the company ordered three twin-screw, 485-foot (148-meter), 5,940-ton (gross) steamers—to be named *Empress of India*, *Empress of Japan*, and *Empress of China*—all to be built at Liverpool. From 1891, when the *Empress of India* left

Cruise by *Canadian Pacific* TO **ALASKA** AND THE **YUKON**

SKAGWAY

JUNEAU

PETERSBURG
WRANGELL

KETCHIKAN

PRINCE RUPERT

OCEAN FALLS

VANCOUVER

VICTORIA

SEATTLE

A brochure describing CPR's Alaska cruise service, circa 1950. The ship depicted is the *Princess Kathleen*. Launched in 1924, it was first used in Vancouver–Victoria–Seattle service, and, during World War II, as a troop carrier. After being returned to Canadian Pacific, it was outfitted for Alaska cruise service. It sank (with no loss of life) after running aground in 1952 while en route from Juneau to Skagway. *Author collection*

Liverpool for the first time en route to Asia, until 1971, when the *Empress of Canada* made its last transatlantic sailing, Canadian Pacific's *Empress* steamers set a high standard for ocean transportation.

After one abortive attempt at entering the coastwise trade in the late 1890s, Canadian Pacific made a more strategic move into this business in 1901 through the purchase of Canadian Pacific Navigation Company and its 14-vessel fleet, which, despite its name, previously had no corporate relationship with CPR. This became the core of CPR's British Columbia Coast Service. As CPR replaced the former C.P.N. fleet with new vessels, the

Princess fleet was born. By 1914, this fleet of 13 vessels was plying routes touching every port between Seattle and Skagway.

CPR had tried for years to reach satisfactory arrangements with existing Atlantic steamship lines for operation of a fast passenger and mail service between Britain and Canada, but to no avail. In 1902, Shaughnessy said that CPR would build its own steamers if it could receive a suitable subsidy for the mail operation. Receiving no response to this proposal, in 1903 CPR entered the

CANADIAN PACIFIC RAILWAY
STEAMSHIP LINES
Atlantic Service
MONTREAL, QUEBEC and LIVERPOOL
For Proposed Sailings see page 58 of this folder
"Taking on the Pilot"
THE EMPRESS OF THE ATLANTIC
EMPRESS OF IRELAND and EMPRESS OF BRITAIN
Finest and Fastest Steamships in the Canadian Service
Hold all Records between Liverpool and Canadian Ports
The two palatial Royal Mail steamships on the Canadian Pacific Railway Company's Atlantic service on the Quebec-Liverpool Route in summer and St. John (N. B.)-Halifax (N. S.)-Liverpool Route in winter. Length 570 feet, breadth 65 feet, 14,500 tons' register, 18,000 horse-power, and make the passage between Liverpool and Quebec in less than a week. Accommodation for 350 1st-cabin, 350 2d-cabin, 1,000 3d-class passengers.
All Canadian Pacific Steamships in the Atlantic service are equipped with Marconi Wireless Telegraphy, and also with a submarine signal system, thus ensuring perfect safety in navigation. The submarine signal acts in foggy weather in the same capacity as a lighthouse does in clear weather.
Detailed Information Will Be Given on Application to
W. B. HOWARD, General Agent, 8 King St., St. John, N. B.
C. L. WILLIAMS, General Agent, 340 Sixth St., Pittsburgh, Pa.
H. M. MacCALLUM, General Agent, 224 South Clark St., Chicago, Ill.
WM. WEBBER, General Agent, Dom. Express Bldg., Montreal, Que.
F. R. PERRY, General Agent, 332 Washington St., Boston, Mass.
A. A. POLHAMUS, General Agent, 609 Spring St., Los Angeles, Cal.
H. M. TAIT, General Agent, 232 Nicollet Ave., Minneapolis, Minn.
I. E. SUCKLING, General Agent, 16 King St., East, Toronto, Ont.
W. H. SNELL, General Agent, 458 Broadway, New York, N. Y.
G. M. JACKSON, General Agent, 645 Market St., San Francisco, Cal.
J. J. FORSTER, General Agent, 713 Second Ave., Seattle, Wash.
J. S. CARTER, General Agent, 210 Portage Ave., Winnipeg, Man.
W. G. ANNABLE, General Passenger Agent, Dominion Express Building, MONTREAL, Que.

This panel from a 1912 CPR timetable depicts the *Empress of Ireland*, one of the company's premier transatlantic steamers. ***Author collection***

Atlantic trade by purchasing 15 relatively young ships from an existing operator. This fleet allowed CPR to implement both a passenger and mail service and a cargo service.

Still, the purchased ships were not as fast as those that CPR had planned to order for its own account—and the standards of speed and vessel size were being raised by the company's main competitor in the Canadian transatlantic service, the Allan Line. In 1904, CPR responded by ordering two vessels, the *Empress of Britain* and the *Empress of Ireland*, which raised the bar a notch with a top speed of 18 to 19 knots. They did not need to be as fast as the fastest ships in service between New York and Britain, because of the shorter distance on the more northerly route. Their fuel consumption and operating performance were efficient enough that CPR was able to operate them without a subsidy for carrying the mail. In 1909, Shaughnessy arranged for CPR to buy control of the Allan Line, eliminating its main competitor on the route. CPR kept the Allan name and did not even acknowledge its control of the line until 1915.

As Lamb summarizes it, "By 1914 the Canadian Pacific had become one of the world's major shipowners. Its ocean, coastal, lake, and river fleets consisted of about a hundred ships, over thirty of them on the Atlantic."

In the aftermath of the war, CPR found it necessary, both because of losses to its prewar fleet and as a way of staying competitive on both oceans, to bolster its fleet with a series of acquisitions. In 1921, it bought four ships, two of which were noteworthy. One of them became the *Empress of Scotland* and was put to work as the flagship of the company's Atlantic fleet. The other became the *Empress of Australia* and went to work on the Pacific, where it was for a time the largest liner of any ownership.

The Allan Line, which CPR had acquired but kept as a separate identity for marketing and operational purposes, was folded into the company's primary fleet during the early 1920s. In 1921, the company's Ocean Services department was given a new identity: Canadian Pacific Steamships Limited.

The Beginnings of Diversification

Having an extensive fleet of oceangoing and lake vessels was not the only way in which CPR distinguished itself from most other North American railways. The company also got into the hotel business very early. CPR began building hotels as a way to avoid moving heavy dining cars up and down grade west of Calgary. The first CPR hotels (Mount Stephen House at Field, Glacier House near Rogers Pass, and Fraser Canyon House at North Bend) began as meal stops for the passengers on CPR trains.

CPR's cash flow was aided by the sale of lots in the new city of Vancouver. Van Horne decided to use some of the proceeds from these real estate dealings to build a new hotel at Banff, Alberta, where hot springs had been discovered in 1883. The location was named by Donald Smith (later Lord Strathcona) for the county in Scotland where George Stephen was born. The hotel, CPR's first other than the original three "meal stop" locations, opened in 1888. The original building was designed by American architect Bruce Price in a château or castle style that would be emulated in other CPR hotels and stations to follow.

In 1893, CPR opened the most imposing of its château-style hotels, the Château Frontenac in Quebec City. Like the Banff Springs

The station at Glacier, British Columbia, in Rogers Pass, looking eastward toward a part of the Selkirks known as the Hermit Range. The photo was taken from CPR's Glacier House hotel. Notman & Son/Library and Archives Canada/C-022331

Hotel and Windsor Station in Montreal, it
was designed by Bruce Price. Between 1901
and 1914, CPR added several new hotels
across Canada and expanded others.

Land was another source of diversification for CPR. As part of its agreement to build
and operate a railway across Canada, Canadian Pacific received a land grant of 25 million
acres (10.1 million hectares). Land served two
main purposes: it could be mortgaged, giving
the railway an infusion of cash to finance
construction, and it could be sold to farmers
willing to develop it, which would put traffic
on the railway.

Unlike railroad land grants in the United
States, which were typically in a checkerboard
pattern adjacent to the right-of-way, CPR's

grant was limited to lands owned by the government, which effectively meant that only
land in the prairie region was included (and
not all of the land, because some of it was set
aside for other purposes). Another limitation,
designed to benefit the railway, was that it
need accept only lands that were suitable for
settlement. The result was that CPR desig-
nated only 5.3 million acres (2.1 million
hectares) adjacent to its main line as part of
the land grant. The balance was to be
obtained in areas far north of the main line
and as far south as the U.S. border.

Although land sales proceeded at a brisk
pace through 1883, in the following years
sales and development were much slower than
the railway's backers had hoped. Drought and

CPR's 1898 station at Vancouver echoed the château style of its major hotels. Designed by brothers Edward and William Maxwell, the attractive structure remained in service only until 1914, when CPR opened a new, larger station in Vancouver. The Maxwell-designed station was then demolished. *Library and Archives Canada/PA-029818*

New York architect Bruce Price was hired by CPR in 1886 to design Windsor Street Station in Montreal. The building was completed in 1889, and new wings were added in 1906 and 1914. The 1914 addition included the 15-story tower shown here, which would serve as the company's headquarters until 1996. *Phil Mason*

economic hard times from the mid-1880s through the mid-1890s stalled the development of the prairies. (One bright spot in the land development picture was in British Columbia, where CPR made a deal with the provincial government for a land grant in 1885. Part of the land included in this grant was on the site where the city of Vancouver now exists. CPR did a brisk business in the

sale of lots in the developing city, which reached a population of 10,000 by 1889.)

In 1897, land sales picked up and in the two-year period 1902–1903 the company's total sales were more than 3.5 million acres (1.4 million hectares), or roughly 10 percent of the 36 million acres (14.6 million hectares) the company had acquired through federal and provincial land grants. Although sales dropped off after that, the company continued to sell land at a steady pace for the next decade. Many of the sales were to immigrants from the United States.

Unfortunately, while CPR's main interest in the land was to see it developed, many buyers had other ideas. Much of the acreage ended up in the hands of speculators who did not occupy or farm their land but simply held it in hope of an eventual profit. Some of those buyers ended up defaulting on their purchases, and CPR reclaimed the land.

CPR was eager to promote settlement in the hot, dry area of southern Alberta. Captain John Palliser, leader of an early expedition into this territory, had warned it would not be hospitable to farming; his forecast proved accurate. Canadian Pacific invested millions of dollars in an elaborate canal system designed to irrigate the territory near Calgary,

using water from the Bow River. Even with the irrigation system in place, settlement of this land remained sparse. Of 1.6 million acres (600,000 hectares) sold in the areas covered by irrigation projects, sales contracts on almost 600,000 acres (240,000 hectares) had to be canceled.

CPR's land ownership would eventually generate a good economic return, but not in the way that the railway's builders had hoped. Much of the land that the company acquired in Alberta proved to have productive oil and gas reserves. When it sold this land, CPR retained mineral, oil, and gas rights, which would be major sources of income for a future Canadian Pacific subsidiary, PanCanadian Petroleum Limited.

Notes with this 1905 photo at Strathmore, Alberta, 35 miles (56 kilometers) east of Calgary, describe it as "a new town, one week old." In fact, the town of Strathmore had been settled soon after the arrival of the Canadian Pacific in 1883, but it was in the dry area of Alberta where poor growing conditions discouraged settlers. By 1905, a CPR-funded irrigation system had reached the town, lots were opened for sale, and Strathmore was moved 4 miles (6.4 kilometers) north. The town later became the site of a 2,000-acre (809-hectare) CPR demonstration farm aimed at showing new settlers how to farm. *Canada Dept. of Mines and Resources/Library and Archives Canada/PA-020553*

This 45-car eastbound freight is close to cresting the summit of Kicking Horse Pass (and the Continental Divide) at Stephen, British Columbia, in August 1938. On the head end are 2-10-2 No. 5810 and 2-8-2 No. 5364, while another 2-10-2, No. 5812, pushes from the rear. *Photo by Otto Perry, Courtesy of Denver Public Library, Western History Collection/OP-20502*

CHAPTER THREE

SERVING CANADA THROUGH PEACE AND WAR: *1918–1948*

During the Shaughnessy years, CPR's route mileage had grown from 7,000 (11,265 kilometers) to 12,993 (20,910). He was succeeded in the presidency of Canadian Pacific by Edward Wentworth Beatty, a man different in several respects from his three predecessors. First, he was Canadian-born. Second, he was a lawyer. Third, he had not participated in the construction of the railway. When the last spike was driven at Craigellachie, he was barely eight years old, and when he became president in 1918, he had just turned 41.

As described by David Cruise and Alison Griffiths, Beatty's 25-year tenure in CPR executive posts (6 as president, 18 as president and chairman, and 1 as chairman) "was radically different from the almost unbroken prosperity of the Shaughnessy years. Beatty's reign began and ended with world wars, and in between he had to cope with dramatic economic swings and the ominous spectre of a new and powerful competitor. J. J. Hill was gone, but the Canadian National Railway Co. more than took his place."

Beatty took over at a time when the economics of the railway were at an inflection point, thanks to the monetary inflation and other economic changes wrought by World War I (in which 1,116 CPR employees died). Since 1900, the company's operating ratio (expenses as a percentage of revenues) had ranged between 60 and 70, except for 1916, when it dipped to 59.7 thanks to the boom in war-related traffic.

In 1918, the year he became president, wage increases and other cost escalation pushed that ratio to 78.1, and for the duration of Beatty's 25 years at the top of the company, the operating ratio never went below 77. His first reaction was to economize. Maintenance was deferred and every operating expense was examined to determine whether it was truly necessary.

CPR could not stand still, however. Equipment was worn out by the crush of traffic it had experienced during the war, and it needed replacement. The only way of achieving long-term operating efficiency on the railway was to modernize it. The company's other businesses, notably ships and hotels, also required investment if Canadian Pacific was to stay ahead of the competition. By the early 1920s, Beatty was ready to move ahead.

Recognizing that CPR would have to wring every possible operating economy out of its infrastructure, Beatty determined that longer, heavier trains were part of the answer to this challenge. To make this possible, he moved quickly to expand CPR's locomotive fleet with an emphasis on heavier, more

A CPR rotary snowplow at Revelstoke, British Columbia, circa 1928. *Canada Dept. of Interior/Library and Archives Canada/ PA-041142*

CPR F1a Jubilee-type 4-4-4 No. 2927 lays overnight at Sutton, Quebec, between runs on the local to Montreal, in December 1955.
Jim Shaughnessy

Handling less-than-carload freight was a labor-intensive business, as shown by this photo taken at Dudswell Junction, Quebec, on CPR's Quebec Central subsidiary, in September 1947. *Photo by Philip Hastings, courtesy of California State Railroad Museum/ negative no. 2606*

powerful engines: 2-8-2 Mikados, 4-6-2 Pacifics, and 2-10-2 Santa Fe types.

At the same time, CPR increased the hauling capacity of its freight cars and raised its track standards. Starting in 1921, 100-pound rail replaced 85-pound as the main-line standard, and in the mountains, 130-pound rail was installed when it became available. Rock ballast, which offered better drainage, replaced gravel.

Many of these steps might have been taken anyway, but they were given special urgency by the presence of a new, nationwide competitor: Canadian National.

Coexisting with Canadian National

CN's leader in the 1920s, Sir Henry Thornton (an American who had been head of the Great Eastern Railway in Britain), was determined to build a company that could compete with CPR on almost every front, including freight and passenger rail services, hotels, and ships.

"Much to Beatty's, and the CPR's, dismay," writes George Buck, "Thornton soon

proved himself capable of turning the CNR into a serious competitor. . . . Beatty spent vast sums to upgrade the CPR both to meet and beat the CNR competition." CPR replaced wooden cars with steel and bought larger and more powerful locomotives.

As a result of this head-to-head competition, both railways invested heavily in new prairie branch lines, with CPR pushing northward into territory where new, more robust varieties of wheat were now being grown. By no coincidence, this was an area that CN (with its east–west routes lying to the north of CPR's) might have considered its own natural preserve. However, CPR had a legitimate interest in developing some of these areas, especially in Alberta, because a portion of its land grant acreage was here. In the period from 1923 to 1931, CPR built 2,121 route miles (3,413 kilometers) of new prairie trackage.

Each player matched or bettered its adversary at every turn. The result was duplication of facilities and services. In the prosperous 1920s, this could be papered over with profits from business where competition didn't drive down prices. But with the onset of the Great Depression in the early 1930s, neither company could afford to play this game any longer.

The Depression, though historically traced to the October 1929 stock market crash, was not immediately evident. In 1930, rail traffic declined but not at an alarming rate. Still, CN, which was dependent on public funds to support its investments in equipment and facilities, and which was still wrestling with the challenge of integrating the varied properties it had inherited, had little margin for error. It had the support of the Liberal government of Mackenzie King, but in 1930 power swung to the Conservatives. Thornton would be answerable for CN's financial results in a way that he had managed to avoid through the boom times of the 1920s.

A June 1925 timetable provides sailing schedules for CPR's Great Lakes steamship services.
Author collection

The issues of competition between private enterprise and public enterprise that Shaughnessy had foreseen during the formative years of Canadian National would now be revisited by Beatty.

In 1931, a Royal Commission was appointed to look into the state of Canada's railways and make recommendations for improvement. They were unsparing in their criticism of CN. Thornton offered only a weak defense of his record. Much of the Commission's criticism of the company related to the lack of private-sector incentives for efficiency, echoing the fears of Shaughnessy as he had watched CNoR and GTP move toward nationalization more than a decade earlier.

Beatty's proposed solution also echoed Shaughnessy. He recommended that CPR and CN be joined together under a single administration, with sufficient financial safeguards to protect the interests of CPR investors. But like his predecessor, he gave too little recognition to the view that many Canadians held of CPR: that it was a potential monopolist that could be checked only by a vigorous competitor.

Acting on the Commission's recommendation that the two national railways be

CP 2822, shown here at Westmount, near Montreal, in March 1957, was a Class H1c Royal Hudson type, delivered by MLW in 1937. Of the 65 H1 Hudsons owned by CPR, 45 were of this semi-streamlined design. After a visit to Canada in 1939 by King George VI and Queen Elizabeth, when the *Royal Train* was hauled by Hudson 2850 from Quebec City to Vancouver, CPR received permission to designate the 45 engines as "Royal Hudsons." The crown on the engine running board symbolized the designation. *Jim Shaughnessy*

forced to cooperate as a means of preventing further financial drain from overeager competition, Parliament in 1933 passed the Canadian National–Canadian Pacific Railway Act. Little came of it. One of the few tangible results was the pooling of passenger trains between Quebec City, Montreal, Ottawa, and Toronto. Another was that CPR closed its hotel in Vancouver and assumed joint control with CN of the new hotel that the latter was building. Beatty continued to press for a unified rail system, but his efforts were in vain.

Ships and Hotels

Thornton made CN competitive with CPR in many ways, but not on the high seas. In this arena, CPR remained the premier Canadian operator. In the late 1920s, Beatty led the company into new investments designed to bolster its competitive position. He was motivated by the operating inefficiencies of some of the vessels acquired after World War I and by changing passenger demographics. A new market was developing among middle-class passengers who wanted something better than steerage but not as expensive as first class. Tourist class was the answer, and in 1928 and 1929 CPR put four *Duchess*-class ships into service to meet this need. They were followed in 1931 by the *Empress of Britain*, the second ship to bear this name, which was meant to serve the first-class market. It was able to make the Quebec–Liverpool roundtrip in just 14 days.

Between 1924 and 1928, CPR engaged in three major hotel projects. The first two, at the Château Lake Louise and Château Frontenac, both involved rebuilding of wings that had been damaged by fire. The third, at Banff Springs, replaced the last parts of the hotel dating to its building in 1887. Other hotel investments followed, most notably the Royal York in Toronto, which opened in 1929, and with a subsequent addition, became the largest hotel in the British Commonwealth.

Whether all the money put into hotels represented a wise investment is open to debate; their return on capital was substantially less than that generated by other parts of the CPR corporate family. Although hotels were always intended to be a sideline—something that would attract travelers to the railway and other CPR transportation services—CN's aggressive hotel-building efforts of the 1920s arguably led CPR to over-invest in this part of its business.

The Crow's Nest Rates: A Growing Problem

The Crow's Nest rates on grain became a source of increasing controversy in the 1920s. Several increases had been authorized during and soon after World War I, and the rate cap had even been suspended during the period from 1919 to 1922. Although operating economies had for a time helped keep the rates compensatory to the railway, postwar inflation in wages and other operating expenses made it increasingly difficult for the railway to make money on this traffic. The grain business was also becoming more complicated because, with the completion of the Panama Canal in 1914, grain from the far West to Europe could now move via Vancouver and the canal at a lower cost than if it were shipped via eastern ports. But the railway faced significant costs in hauling grain over several mountain ranges to reach the Pacific.

The Banff Springs Hotel reopened in 1928, following an extensive rebuilding, with 600 rooms. This photo was taken soon after the project was completed. *Photo by W. J. Oliver, courtesy of Glenbow Archives/NA-4868-277*

CP 5915, a Class T1a 2-10-4 Selkirk type built by MLW in 1929, is shown at Banff, Alberta, in August 1938. The Selkirks were designed under the supervision of Henry Bowen, who served as CPR's chief of motive power from 1928 to 1949. Historian Omer Lavallée notes that the Selkirk type was "the largest and heaviest steam locomotive to operate in the British Commonwealth during Canada's steam era." The 20 T1a Selkirks were assigned to main-line and helper service between Calgary and Revelstoke. *Photo by Otto Perry, Courtesy of Denver Public Library, Western History Collection/OP-20417*

By the 1920s the Crow's Nest rate had already become an article of faith among Canadian farmers; in a business subject to the vagaries of weather and an unpredictable marketplace, stable transportation rates helped keep them in business even as the price of grain itself fluctuated from year to year. For the next five decades and more, railway rates on grain would be a subject of continuing dialogue, controversy, and friction involving the growers, their political representatives, and the railways.

Surviving the Depression

In the United States, many railroads were forced into bankruptcy during the Depression, including all four of CPR's U.S. subsidiaries (Soo Line, Duluth, South Shore & Atlantic, Wisconsin Central, and Spokane International).

CPR was able to avoid bankruptcy. For years, it had sought capital through issuance of stock whenever possible, rather than by issuing debt, making it more robust than many of its U.S. counterparts. It did suspend its dividend for a time, but that was a small price for shareholders to pay, given the alternative of having their investment wiped out in bankruptcy court.

CPR's second source of strength was its physical plant. Though operated conservatively, CPR's management had consistently worked to improve the condition of the road's equipment and track. The 1920s had been a

CP 2928 is a Class F1a 4-4-4. A 1938 product of the CLC shop at Kingston, Ontario, it has been preserved by the Canadian Railroad Historical Association at Delson, Quebec, where this photo was taken in 1972. The CRHA describes the engine as follows: "CP 2928 represents the 'Jubilee' wheel arrangement, light motive power designed by Bowen for service on secondary lines. The wheel arrangement was peculiar to the CPR in Canada and was developed to replace the older, smaller locomotives used on these lines."
Jim Shaughnessy

time of particularly vigorous efforts to improve the property. Thus, maintenance expenses could be cut back for a time without putting the railway's employees, passengers, or shippers at risk.

Although it was financially and physically stronger than many other railways, CPR had to engage in serious belt-tightening to survive the Depression. Employment fell from 75,709 people in 1928 to 49,412 in 1933. Wages of railway operating employees were cut from their original levels in 1933, first by 10 percent and then by 20 percent. These wage cuts were reversed in stages between 1935 and 1938.

Another set of contributors to CPR's relative success during the Depression was its various non-rail operations. Hotels, ships, and the smelter at Trail, British Columbia, all earned operating profits during this period, which helped the parent company weather the economic adversity of this decade.

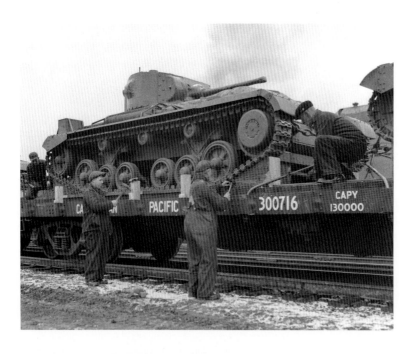

In World War II (as in World War I) CPR shops were converted to produce munitions. By the end of 1943, CPR's Angus Shops in Montreal had built 1,420 28-ton Valentine tanks. This shipment, being secured to railcars on December 29, 1941, was en route to the Soviet Union. *National Film Board of Canada/Library and Archives Canada/PA-174520*

Pushing the Railway to Its Limits: World War II

The beginning of Beatty's tenure as president of Canadian Pacific came shortly before the end of World War I. His service in this post would conclude as World War II began. By 1940, his health limited his participation in the affairs of the company, and many of his duties were assumed by vice president D'Alton C. Coleman, who had earlier served as vice president in the company's western region. In 1942, Coleman became president, and Beatty died the following year.

Between 1918, when Beatty became president, and 1943, when he died, CPR had grown from 12,993 route miles (20,910 kilometers) to 17,034 (27,414). Much of this growth resulted from the addition of more than 2,000 miles (3,200 kilometers) of branch line on the prairies. CPR's all-time peak Canadian mileage was attained in 1936: 17,241 miles (27,747 kilometers).

The onset of war in Europe, and Britain's growing involvement in it, was reflected in a pickup in CPR's traffic. Revenue ton-miles, which approached 15 billion in 1929, and then fell below 10 billion in 1933, grew to more than 16 billion in 1940. At the peak of the war effort, in 1944, volumes topped out at more than 27 billion revenue ton-miles.

As in the first World War, Canadian Pacific's first direct involvement with the war effort came through the takeover of its ocean-going fleet. "By the spring of 1940," W. Kaye Lamb writes, "eighteen of the company's twenty ocean liners and freighters had been taken over, and one [the freighter *Beaverburn*] had been lost. . . . The loss was the first of many, for few shipping companies were to suffer as high a proportion of fleet casualties as the Canadian Pacific." An early casualty of the war was the 42,000-ton *Empress of Britain*, which was serving as a transport. On October 26, 1940, it was attacked by German aircraft off the coast of Ireland; it sank two days later. Beatty took the news of this loss very

CP 7014 was part of CPR's first group of production-model diesel locomotives, five American Locomotive Company (Alco) S-2 units delivered in 1943. Prior to the delivery of these locomotives, CPR's only diesel locomotive was a one-of-a-kind switch engine built by National Steel Car Company of Hamilton, Ontario, using British components. In February 1968, CP 7014 is about to exchange cabooses on the rear of an eastbound freight at Farnham, Quebec. At the time, cabooses ("vans" in Canadian parlance) were assigned to individual crews. CP 7014 remained on the CPR roster until 1982. *Bill Linley*

hard, since the ship was not only the pride of the fleet, but also his personal favorite.

"Six *Empresses*, four *Duchesses*, and five *Beavers* steamed a total of 3,617,000 miles (5,821,000 kilometers) and carried over a million military and civilian passengers and about a million tons of cargo. The cost," Lamb writes, "was high; by the end of the war eleven of the fifteen ships had been lost, nine by enemy action and two by marine accident."

CPR's traffic was bolstered at first by the shortage of shipping capacity, which put freight on the railway that would have otherwise moved via water. The port of Saint John became much busier, as vessel operators sought to avoid the longer cruises that calls at Montreal or Quebec City would have required. Halifax saw a similar surge, but it was served by CN; CPR's Dominion Atlantic was not a significant factor there.

Aside from the growth in freight traffic, CPR's passenger business was also swollen by both military and civilian traffic. In 1941, the company carried 9.1 million passengers. In 1944, it carried an all-time record 18.5 million.

A 1946 company publication recorded the cost of war to CPR's employees: "Over 20,000 C.P.R. people answered the call to the colors and of that number 658 were killed on active service."

The aftermath of World War II was similar to that of World War I. Inflation in wages and prices drove up the railway's operating expenses, while government control over rail rates, and the inevitable decline in volumes

CP 5313 leads a doubleheaded westbound freight crossing the St. Francis River at Lennoxville, just east of Sherbrooke, Quebec, in January 1954. The 5313 was a Class P2b 2-8-2 Mikado built by MLW in 1920.
Jim Shaughnessy

once the war effort wound down, created a squeeze on operating income. In the postwar era, labor was unwilling to abide the company's paternalistic attitude of earlier generations. They wanted higher wages, as well as working conditions more on a par with those in other industries. A strike in 1950 resulted in the appointment of an arbitrator who granted the operating unions both a wage increase and a reduction in the normal work week to 40 hours.

Limited availability of new equipment during the war meant that cars and locomo-tives, which had been taxed to their limit during the war, needed repair and replacement. The competitive landscape was also changing, with airlines, truckers, and the automobile all competing for a slice of the railway's business.

Coleman saw Canadian Pacific through the war years and retired in 1947, at age 68. His place as chairman and president of the company was taken by William M. Neal, who would serve in the post for only one year. When Neal retired in 1948, the functions of chairman and president were split, with G. A.

Walker taking over as chairman and William A. Mather as president.

But the appointment that would have the most dramatic long-term implications for the railway was that of Norris R. "Buck" Crump as vice president of the railway in 1948. Crump started his CPR career in his hometown of Revelstoke, British Columbia, at the age of 16. He took leaves of absence to obtain first a bachelor's and then, in 1936, a master's degree, both at Purdue University in Indiana. His master's thesis was about potential railway applications of the internal-combustion engine.

CPR had been slow to adopt the diesel-electric engine, and when Crump moved to his new position, the conventional wisdom among most senior managers was that the diesel's primary role would be in the yard, not on the road. Crump brought a different perspective to the steam-versus-diesel issue. Over the next 12 years, CPR would undergo a radical change in the way it powered its freight and passenger trains.

An eastbound doubleheaded CPR freight at Lennoxville, Quebec, on the Montreal–Saint John line, on a minus-20-degree Fahrenheit day in January 1954. *Jim Shaughnessy*

A westbound train, with MLW RS-3 CP 8444 leading, enters the Belleville Subdivision at Smith Falls, Ontario, in December 1965. *Bill Linley*

THE CRUMP ERA:
1948–1972

Norris Crump held the presidency of Canadian Pacific from 1955 to 1964; during the last three years of this term he also held the position of chairman. After the premature death of his successor as president, Robert A. Emerson, he held both posts again for a short time in 1966, until Ian D. Sinclair was named president. Crump continued as chairman until his retirement in 1972, when Sinclair took over as chairman and Frederick S. Burbidge became president.

In November 1954, the local train from Sutton, Quebec, to Montreal, pulled by Jubilee (Class F1a) 4-4-4 2927, passes a pair of diesels led by Alco FA-1 4006 on a freight bound for Newport, Vermont, at West Brome, Quebec. *Jim Shaughnessy*

Although Crump's term as president amounted to less than ten years, the entire period from 1948 to 1972 can fairly be called "The Crump Era." He was the person who set in motion two major forces that irrevocably changed Canadian Pacific: the technological modernization of the railway and the broad diversification of the company's business portfolio, both within and outside the transportation industry. During the last six years of Crump's time with Canadian Pacific, his successor, Ian Sinclair, became the public face of the company and further broadened the company's business portfolio, but Sinclair was implementing ideas that had started with Crump.

The End of Steam and the Beginning of Dieselization

When Crump arrived at headquarters in 1948, CPR was still acquiring steam locomotives. The last new steam locomotive

delivered to the railway arrived in March 1949. It was a 2-10-4 Selkirk, No. 5935, assigned to operate between Calgary and Revelstoke, and while it was in many respects the pinnacle of CPR steam locomotive development, it had a short career, lasting only until 1956.

As the last steam power was arriving on the scene, so were the first diesels. Between 1943 and 1947, the company had purchased 55 diesels for yard service. In 1949, it took two additional steps on the path toward dieselization. The Esquimalt & Nanaimo, CPR's Vancouver Island operation, received a

Steam and diesel were serviced side-by-side at the St. Luc Yard engine house in Montreal, and at dozens of other CPR locations, throughout the transition period of the middle and late 1950s. The two forms of motive power are represented here by Class G1s 4-6-2 2210 (built by CPR in 1907) and FA-2 4091, a 1953 product of MLW. Dieselization of the railway would be completed in 1960. *Jim Shaughnessy*

group of Baldwin road switchers that allowed steam operations to be phased out. In the East, three General Motors (Electro-Motive Division) E8's went into service as part of an equipment pool with the Boston & Maine Railroad, powering passenger trains between Montreal and Boston. Freight operations in

By Train...
THROUGH THE
Canadian Rockies
THE
CANADIAN PACIFIC
WAY

Class T1c Selkirk 5935, shown here on a CPR booklet describing the railway's route through the Rockies, was the last Canadian Pacific steam locomotive delivered, on March 12, 1949. Both the ten T1b Selkirks delivered in 1938 and the final six Class T1c engines of 1949 were semi-streamlined, carried Tuscan red side panels and gold-leaf trim, and were assigned to passenger trains between Calgary and Revelstoke. CP 5935 has been preserved by the Canadian Railroad Historical Association as part of its collection at Delson, Quebec. *Author collection*

In 1905, CPR purchased the Esquimalt & Nanaimo Railway on Vancouver Island for $1 million. CPR then expanded the railway from 78 miles (125 kilometers) to approximately 200 miles (320 kilometers). The railway's traffic base consisted almost entirely of forest products. To reach the mainland, freight cars moved via the ferry slip at Nanaimo, shown here in 1970. Baldwins 8000 and 8001 (Model DRS4-4-1000) were CPR's first road switchers, part of a group of 13 units delivered in 1948 to dieselize the E&N. *Steve Patterson*

Vermont and southern Quebec, and on the north shore of Lake Superior, were the next to be dieselized.

Dieselization had to accommodate two main needs: the training of personnel (both operating crews and maintenance workers) and the development of facilities to fuel and maintain the new locomotives. Because of these factors, diesels were first introduced on a region-by-region basis. Later, as enough territories had the trained staff and the facilities to deal with diesels, certain trains were dieselized across several divisions. Steam operations were eliminated completely in 1960.

Aside from the conversion to diesel power, the railway was modernized in many other ways in the decade following World War II. In addition to automatic block signals that were installed on more than 3,000 miles (4,800 kilometers) of the railway, more than 31,000 new freight cars were added to the CPR fleet, and in 1950 a new classification yard was opened at St. Luc, west of Montreal, equipped with retarders and automatic switch controls.

One of CPR's early ventures into dieselization involved its Montreal–Boston passenger service, operated jointly with the Boston & Maine. B&M assigned EMD E7 diesels to the trains, and CPR wanted to assign similar units to the power pool for these trains. By the time CPR placed its order, the improved E8 model was available, and CP specified the newer design. Here, CP 1802, one of the railway's three E8 units, powers the daytime *Alouette* as it approaches Glencliff Summit, New Hampshire, on the B&M in May 1950. *Photo by Philip Hastings, courtesy of California State Railroad Museum/negative no. 800*

Squeezed Between Rising Costs and Regulated Rates

As much as CPR needed a technological overhaul, the program carried out under Crump's leadership in the years before he became president was a costly one. According to W. Kaye Lamb, "modernization, which had begun in 1947 and under Crump's urging had been stepped up to an intensive five-year program in 1951, had cost $600 million by the time he assumed the presidency in 1955. . . . It had been a difficult period financially."

David Cruise and Alison Griffiths add more color to the picture, noting that when Crump became president, he "inherited the CPR's highest debt since 1941, the highest fixed charges since 1948 and the lowest return on investment since 1922. The source of the problems was the railroad itself . . . Crump faced a classic Catch 22: the railroad couldn't attract investment because it wasn't profitable and couldn't become profitable without massive investment. And there was a devilish kicker, the notorious 1897 Crow Rate . . . which froze grain rates—the largest component of rail revenue—at artificially low levels."

Costs continued to escalate, but increases in freight rates could not keep pace. The most worrisome source of cost increases, because it represented a very large percentage of operating

Above: In the early 1960s, service on the Montreal–Boston route was converted to Budd Rail Diesel Cars, freeing CPR's E8 units for other service. In June 1968, CP 1802 is on a Quebec City train about to depart Montreal's Windsor Station. At right is Canadian Pacific's Château Champlain hotel, opened in 1967. *Jim Shaughnessy* **Left:** CPR began to dieselize its freight service between Montreal and Wells River, Vermont, in May 1949, with the acquisition of twelve 1,500-horsepower road-freight units (eight FA-1 cab units and four FB-1 booster units) from Alco. The fresh paint is visible on this FA-1 as the engineer removes white flags from the unit at Wells River, the interchange point with the Boston & Maine, approximately two months after the FA-1s were delivered. *Photo by Philip Hastings, courtesy of California State Railroad Museum/ negative no. 2521*

In 1949, CPR received five Alco RS-2 road switchers. For most of their careers they were assigned out of Newport, Vermont, or Brownville Junction, Maine. In February 1977, CP 8403 is at Richford, Vermont. *George Pitarys*

expenses, was labor. Union negotiators were becoming more demanding and less willing to settle for what they considered substandard wages and working conditions.

If CPR's unions were becoming more demanding, so were the company's shippers. Rail rates were (and are) set, in large measure, by what the market can bear. That meant that western shippers, with few competitive options, typically paid higher freight rates on commodities like lumber and minerals than their eastern counterparts did on manufactured goods, which could move by either truck or rail.

A Royal Commission was appointed in 1948 to look into the question of how Canada's national transportation policy should deal with the competing interests of shippers and railways. There were rhetorical concessions to the company's need for an adequate return on capital. However, the results of the Commission's work, as implemented by the Board of Transport Commissioners (the body that regulated rail rates), was a formula for calculating a fair return that, from CPR's perspective, left much to be desired. CPR felt that it needed a return of 6 percent or more in order to justify the ongoing reinvestment in plant and equipment that would keep the railroad alive; actual returns in the period 1953–1955 were between 2 and 3 percent.

The compression between wages that rose with each new round of negotiations, and freight rates that could never be increased enough to offset inflation, led the railway to focus on productivity. Crump's modernization replaced labor with capital: diesels could haul more tonnage with less maintenance than steam engines; Centralized Traffic Control that allowed the elimination of train order operators at remote stations; computer systems that mechanized the work formerly done by rooms full of clerks; and track machinery that reduced the labor involved in right-of-way maintenance. The result was a

From the photographer's notes: "The CPR local at Teeswater, Ontario, at the end of a wandering branch in southern Ontario, on the last day of mixed train passenger service." This photo was taken on August 2, 1957. The 83-mile (134-kilometer) line branched off the Toronto–Owen Sound line at Orangeville, which is where this mixed train originated. *Jim Shaughnessy*

At Vallée Junction, Quebec, in May 1959, the baggageman on the Quebec Central local from Lac Frontier unloads shipments for transfer to a Quebec City-bound train. *Jim Shaughnessy*

dramatic decline in the railway's labor force from its peak of 83,848 workers in 1952 to 57,778 in 1962. It would see further declines in the years ahead.

One particular issue addressed during Crump's tenure was the question of firemen on diesel locomotives. At its simplest level, the dispute centered on the railway's assertion that firemen were not necessary to the safe operation of diesels. The union representing these employees, the Brotherhood of Locomotive Firemen and Enginemen, said that they were. Following strikes in 1956 and 1958, and the appointment of a Royal Commission (under Justice R. L. Kellock), CPR ultimately implemented a policy of eliminating firemen's positions through attrition.

Even though it had substantially cut its labor force, CPR complained to regulators that it was not earning an adequate return on capital. In 1959, Regina lawyer M. A. McPherson was appointed to chair another Royal Commission charged with investigating the economic situation of the railways. In a series of findings, the Commission said, first, that the railways should be relieved of the burden imposed by the low level of grain rates under the Crow's Nest Pass Agreement. Second, the Commission said that the government's economic regulation of the railways should be relaxed, though not eliminated. It would be a long time before this recommendation would have any tangible effect, but it was a start.

The National Transportation Act of 1967 took several important steps toward relaxing the rigid regulatory framework under which Canadian railways operated. One step toward greater market freedom was the ability to publish multicar rates, which encouraged the development of unit trains. The first such train in Canada was a 1967 movement of sulfuric acid from Copper Cliff, Ontario, on CPR, to Sarnia, Ontario, on CN. Three years later, coal began to move in trainload quantities

In February 1966, CPR Train 951 digs in while leaving the yard at Smiths Falls, Ontario, with a tonnage westbound train on a very cold morning in February 1966. The train is en route to Winnipeg, Manitoba. Leading this train is CP 4050, an MLW FA-2, delivered in 1951. It was scrapped in 1977. *Bill Linley*

from mines in southeastern British Columbia to the Roberts Bank terminal near Vancouver for export to Japan. The movement of coal soon became a major source of revenue for CPR.

Still, even with some market freedoms, the Crow Rates on grain were a significant constraint. By CPR's reckoning, these rates were below cost. Given the poor economics of moving grain, both CPR and CN cut back on their investments in the business. Even while U.S. railroads were converting to 100-ton covered hoppers, Canadian grain moved in 40-foot boxcars with a capacity of 70 tons or less. In the early 1970s, the Canadian government stepped in to provide 6,000 modern covered hopper cars, assigning some to each major railway. But this was not a complete solution.

Diversification Picks up Steam

One reality of the postwar years was that trucking became an important factor in the movement of freight. Canadian Pacific took steps to add trucking to its portfolio of services, through the formation of Canadian Pacific Transport Limited in 1947. The services offered by CP Transport were largely an adjunct to the company's rail service, providing off-line customers with a way of moving their goods to and from rail-served stations.

Piggyback (trailer-on-flatcar, or TOFC) service was initiated in December 1952, meaning that goods once placed in a trailer by the shipper did not have to be transloaded into boxcars in order to take advantage of the economies of line-haul rail service. They could stay in the trailer from origin to destination, with over-the-road service provided by truckers at both ends of the movement. In 1958, CPR acquired Smith Transport Limited, at the time Canada's largest trucker, and it soon became commonplace to see Smith trailers moving across Canada by rail.

Diversification took another significant step forward with the formation in 1962 of Canadian Pacific Investments Limited, which became the company's vehicle for ownership and management of non-transportation ventures. It started with Canadian Pacific's existing

In July 1966, MLW C-424 CP 4242 leads Train 903 just west of Smiths Falls, Ontario, on the Belleville Subdivision. *Bill Linley*

Photographer Bill Linley's notes state that "commuter train 250 with 1600-horsepower MLW RS-10 8472 awaits the highball at 9:45 A.M. on Wednesday June 1, 1965. Six more station stops will be made by the time the 9.5-mile (15.3-kilometer) run is completed at Montreal's Windsor Station. CPR rostered 66 of these versatile locomotives, which were a Canada-only model that superseded the RS-3. Forty-six RS-10 units such as the 8472 were boiler-equipped for dual service, as signified by the nose-mounted beaver shield, and they powered many eastern passenger runs throughout the 1960s." *Bill Linley*

oil and gas subsidiary, plus a timber operation. It soon added Consolidated Mining and Smelting Company (later shortened to Cominco), the company's hotels, and a real estate unit, Marathon Realty.

By branching out into non-transportation businesses, Canadian Pacific followed a popular trend among North American railways, but it had an advantage: most of these operating units did not require acquisition or new investment, but simply a reorganization and a redefinition of their relationship to the parent company. They were no longer ancillary to the railway, but succeeded or failed on their own ability to compete in their respective markets.

Over time, CP Investments extended its reach beyond the original holdings. The oil and gas and timber units both added to their original properties. Hotels were built in new locations, including some overseas cities, and new operating units were added, including Great Lakes Paper, a part interest in forest products and paper producer MacMillan Bloedel, and a controlling interest in Algoma Steel.

When unit coal train service began from southern British Columbia to Roberts Bank, near Vancouver, the cars supplied by CPR were painted red, as shown in this August 1970 photo of an 803 train on the Windermere Subdivision, led by MLW M-630 4552. The cars soon turned black from coal dust, and by 1972 the railway conceded defeat. All new coal cars from that time forward were delivered in black paint. *Stan Smaill*

A coal train is loaded on the loop track at the Kaiser Balmer loadout at Elkview, British Columbia, in August 1975. *Phil Mason*

Most diesel locomotives are actually diesel-electrics, but CP 23, shown here at Vallée Junction, Quebec, in August 1964, was a rare exception: a diesel-hydraulic, or more specifically, a diesel-torque-convertor locomotive. CPR had a handful of these small units, and CP 23 was in fact part of the last group of locomotives built for a Canadian railway by Canadian Locomotive Company of Kingston, Ontario: five 44-ton D-T-C units, delivered in 1960. Here, it switches a local that has just arrived from Lac Frontier. *Jim Shaughnessy*

CP Investments also became involved in the coal business in the early 1970s through a venture known as Fording Coal. The company had owned land in southeastern British Columbia with known coal deposits since 1909, but they were not considered economical to develop. In the 1960s, nearby deposits were acquired by Kaiser Resources Limited, which sold the coal to Japanese steel mills, moving it in unit trains through the port of Vancouver. This encouraged Canadian Pacific to take a closer look at its own coal interest in the region. The result was Fording.

Reflecting the reduced role of the railway in generating earnings for the company's shareholders, in 1971 the corporate name was formally changed to Canadian Pacific Limited. This was hard for some longtime employees and other stakeholders to accept, but it was symbolic of the fact that the company had been foresighted enough to spread its bets around. If the company had been forced to stand or fall on the financial results of the railway alone, it is doubtful that it would have weathered the economic pressures of the postwar years as well as it did.

Canadian Pacific Enters the Airline Business

CPR had been given an opportunity to become a part-owner of Trans-Canada Airlines (later Air Canada) during the 1930s. It declined because of the limited control it would have over the airline, but it remained interested in adding air services to its portfolio. Canadian Pacific Air Lines came into existence in 1942. Its assets included the employees, aircraft, and facilities of ten small airlines that the company had acquired during 1941. The war gave the nascent airline an opportunity to participate in ferrying aircraft across the Atlantic and from Canada to Alaska, and in the training of pilots for military service. It was restricted from competing with Trans-

CPR had 21 Fairbanks-Morse-designed Train Masters (Model H24-66): former demonstrator 8900, built in 1955 by F-M at Beloit, Wisconsin, and 20 units delivered in 1956, all built to F-M's design by CLC. Although they were used at various locations during their careers, by the 1970s they were concentrated in two places: Montreal and Tadanac Yard near Trail, British Columbia. Here, CP 8917 rides high on the St. Lawrence River Bridge as it sets off cars in the yard at LaSalle, Quebec. *Stan Smaill*

Canada, but Canadian Pacific Air Lines found a niche in regional services, primarily in the West but also in eastern Canada.

In 1948, the government authorized Canadian Pacific to begin air service across the Pacific. The company intended to serve China, Japan, and Australia. Service began in 1949 using Canadair Four aircraft, a Canadian version of the Douglas DC-4. China was

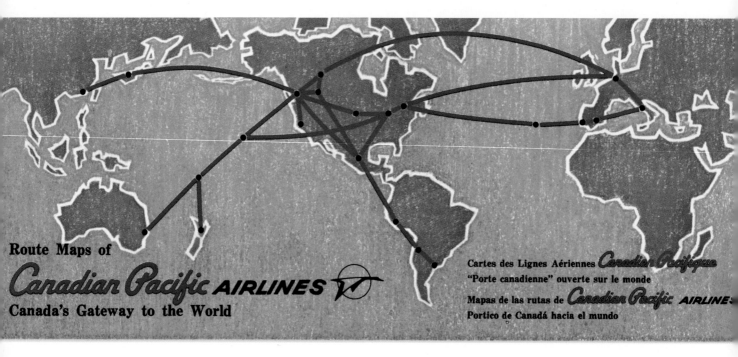

Route Maps of
Canadian Pacific AIRLINES
Canada's Gateway to the World

Cartes des Lignes Aériennes *Canadian Pacifique*
"Porte canadienne" ouverte sur le monde
Mapas de las rutas de *Canadian Pacific* AIRLINES
Portico de Canadá hacia el mundo

A 1960s map of Canadian Pacific Airlines' domestic and international routes. *Author collection*

quickly dropped as a destination when the Communists came to power. However, the company's Tokyo service proved to be a great success.

In the early 1950s, the fleet was updated with Convair planes for domestic routes and Douglas DC-6s for international routes. Vancouver became the operational hub of the growing airline, which started service to Mexico and Peru in 1953. Two years later, service to Amsterdam via the polar route began, and soon after a Toronto–Mexico City route was inaugurated.

Although the airline struggled financially in the late 1950s and early 1960s, Crump was confident enough about its long-term prospects to support the acquisition of DC-8 jet aircraft in 1961. With faster, more comfortable aircraft, the airline was able to cultivate the international travel market and go from red ink to black by the mid-1960s.

It expanded its jet fleet with stretched DC-8s and Boeing 737s in the late 1960s, and in 1973 it invested in 747s to serve its long-distance routes. By the mid-1970s the airline served Japan, China, Australia, Hawaii, Mexico, Peru, Chile, Argentina, the

Netherlands, Portugal, Spain, Italy, Greece, and Israel. It continued to serve destinations in western Canada, and although required by the government to play second fiddle to Air Canada, it had a modest presence in cross-Canada markets.

The Last Stand of the Passenger Liners

Steamship services were restored slowly after the war, in part because the government was slow to release the remaining vessels from the company's prewar fleet. Like the railway, the ship line found itself in a new environment after the war, and eventually Canadian Pacific decided that it would restore passenger service only on the Atlantic, since airline service seemed likely to siphon off business from its Pacific routes. By the summer of 1950, three *Empress* vessels were serving the transatlantic trade (and doing cruise duty in the off-season). In 1956, the company began to order ships to reequip this service.

Between 1955 and 1961, the company acquired three new vessels for the summer transatlantic trade and the winter cruise business: a new *Empress of Britain*, followed soon

For a world of service...
travel *Canadian Pacific*

Across Canada...from the picturesque East Coast...to the inspiring Canadian Rockies and the evergreen playground on the Pacific Coast ...Canadian Pacific trains carry you smoothly, comfortably.

Enjoy the finest in travel comfort...modern equipment...friendly service...superb meals ...all these are yours when you travel The Canadian Pacific Way.

Sea to Sea...on Canada's West Coast in Victoria, B.C., visit the gracious Empress Hotel, or any of Canadian Pacific's 18 other hotels and lodges from sea to sea. The Canadian Pacific is your host in many of Canada's great cities... in the magnificent Canadian Rockies... beside the mighty St. Lawrence...on the colorful East Coast.

As you travel across Canada you are never more than 24 hours from a Canadian Pacific hotel.

Across the Pacific...fly Canadian Pacific style to Australia and the Far East.

Enjoy the same high standard of Canadian Pacific service in the air as on land or sea when you fly pressurized "EMPRESS" aircraft from Vancouver via Honolulu and Fiji to Australia. From Vancouver via Alaska to Tokyo and Hong Kong you will fly the shortest and fastest air route to the Orient.

Canadian Pacific

SPANS THE WORLD
RAILWAYS • STEAMSHIPS
AIR LINES • HOTELS
COMMUNICATIONS • EXPRESS

by the *Empress of England* and, in 1961, the largest of the three, the *Empress of Canada*. Beginning in the mid-1960s, however, the company yielded to the reality that airlines had replaced steamships as the preferred method of travel between Canada and Britain. By the 1971 summer season, only the *Empress of Canada* remained, and by the end of the year it, too, had made its last voyage under the Canadian Pacific flag.

The company remained actively involved in cargo shipping and successfully made the transition from break-bulk methods of handling freight to the new and far more efficient style of international shipping: containerization. Not only did containers reduce port labor and improve vessel utilization, but inland transportation for shippers located significant

On the back cover of its October 1949 timetable, Canadian Pacific advertises both its airline and its hotels, in addition to its rail passenger service. *Author collection*

12 vacation treats
White Empress style to Europe
go Canadian Pacific for service!

1: Europe awaits you! Sail there in luxurious White Empress Cruise style. **2:** The only sheltered Trans-Atlantic route—⅓ the way down the St. Lawrence River—with 1000 miles of sight-seeing.

3: Six or seven days to relax and have shipboard fun between Montreal and Liverpool. **4:** An ocean vacation with the satisfaction of real thrift. First-class Empress luxury from $230. Tourist comfort from $152, depending on ship and season.

5: Make new friends among the discriminating people who sail Empress style. **6:** Active fun: deck sports, swimming. **7:** Social games. **8:** The comfort of attended children's rooms.

9: Airy staterooms for perfect rest! **10:** The Captain's dinner, grand climax of Empress hospitality. **11:** Gourmet meals, dancing every night, movies. **12:** And 'round the clock, the blessing of Canadian Pacific's skilled, courteous service.

Ask your travel agent about a world of Canadian Pacific service. Canadian Pacific trains across Canada. Your choice of 19 hotels and resorts. Cruises to Alaska. Airliners to the Far East, New Zealand and Australia.

Canadian Pacific

See your local agent or Canadian Pacific in principal cities in U.S. and Canada.

The *Empress of Scotland* is depicted in an advertisement from the mid-1950s. Originally the *Empress of Japan*, the vessel was used in transpacific service from 1930 to 1939, and then as a troop ship from late 1939 until 1948. It entered transatlantic and cruise service in 1950, and remained in service for Canadian Pacific through the 1957 transatlantic season, at the end of which it was sold to the Hamburg-Atlantic line. *Author collection*

distances from ports was typically by rail. In 1970 and 1971, three new ships were delivered, all of them designed specifically to handle containers. In Canada, they served the port of Quebec (through the Wolfe's Cove terminal) and in Europe they called weekly at Rotterdam, London, and LeHavre.

Through a separate subsidiary, Canadian Pacific (Bermuda) Limited, the company entered another steamship market, this one involving the transportation of petroleum and other bulk commodities. Throughout the late 1960s and into the 1970s, this unit built up a fleet of tankers and other vessels that far

In May 1971, the eastbound *Canadian* pauses at the former Fort William station in Thunder Bay, Ontario. The passenger standing near the door of the sleeping car is en route to Montreal, where she will board Canadian Pacific's *Empress of Canada* to sail to England; this would be the last season for the company's transatlantic passenger services. Grain is delivered by rail to the massive Saskatchewan Wheat Pool elevator, and then shipped out on Great Lakes vessels. *Tom Murray*

outranked the container fleet in terms of sheer tonnage. In addition, the company continued to provide coastal passenger services through vessels based at Vancouver, as well as a Bay of Fundy service between Saint John, New Brunswick, and Digby, Nova Scotia.

The dome seating of the observation car *Algonquin Park* on the westbound *Canadian* appears quite full, as a rainbow appears on the south side of the train, at Field, British Columbia, in June 1975. *Steve Patterson*

CPR's Passenger Trains

Today, Canadian Pacific Railway is freight only, except where it hosts passenger trains operated by VIA Rail Canada, Amtrak, private companies (such as Rocky Mountaineer Vacations), and government-sponsored commuter authorities. The railway does operate a limited cruise-type service, the Royal Canadian Pacific, based in Calgary, and, on an irregular basis, special trains designed to enhance the company's community relations efforts. Such services are, no doubt, important to their users, but they are not part of the railway's core business.

Canadian Pacific has always taken pride in its history. In 2000, it inaugurated a luxury train service, the Royal Canadian Pacific, using restored heavyweight cars and locomotives in the historic CPR grey and Tuscan red livery. Although the train's normal route takes it on a loop from Calgary west to Golden, British Columbia, then south through the Crowsnest Pass, and back to Calgary, it occasionally ventures to other points on the CPR system. Here, it departs Revelstoke, British Columbia, westbound in August 2000. On the rear is the dining car *Mount Stephen*, originally built as a venue for meetings of the Canadian Pacific board of directors. *Phil Mason*

However, for the first 80-plus years of Canadian Pacific's existence, passenger service was an integral part of its daily operations. CPR did not just operate passenger trains: it provided a totality of passenger services unmatched by any other North American railway, including lake, coastal, and transoceanic steamers, and hotels that set high standards in both architecture and amenities. Management did not consider passenger service an afterthought, but a central part of what the company did.

Transcontinental Service

The most visible part of CPR's passenger train network was its transcontinental service. In the company's early years, this service focused on two things: scenery and settlement. Any railway across western Canada would have found itself traversing the Rocky Mountains and the river canyons of British Columbia, but the decision of CPR's founders to push through Kicking Horse Pass and over the Selkirk Mountains gave this railway a spectacular array of natural attractions to lure passengers onto its trains. One of

William Van Horne's most oft-repeated quotations was, "If we can't export the scenery, we will import the tourists."

Van Horne, in fact, was the driving force behind CPR's investment in resort hotels. The CPR dining halls at Laggan (Lake Louise), Field, and Glacier soon added lodging. Van Horne, always eager to exploit new business opportunities, saw that by turning these accommodations into destinations, Canadian Pacific could build a clientele of relatively well-to-do urban dwellers who wanted to be pampered while taking in the natural beauty of British Columbia and western Alberta. That's exactly what Canadian Pacific did at its western resorts, the most famous of which became Château Lake Louise and Banff Springs Hotel.

CPR had another market to serve with its long-distance trains, one that would prove just as important to the company's long-term health. That market was the settler, the immigrant, the farmer relocating to western Canada. "Colonization" was the term used to describe this process, and the railway devoted considerable energy to recruiting people who

Right: Two adjacent panels from a November 1919 CPR timetable cover are aimed at the principal markets for the company's transcontinental passenger services: immigrants interested in settling in the West and those who could afford to indulge themselves at the company's hotels, such as the Empress in Victoria. *Author collection* **Below:** An August 1899 advertisement for CPR's new transcontinental train, the *Imperial Limited. Author collection*

would gamble on starting a new life in a territory they had never seen. Some of the settlers came from the European continent, some from Ireland, and some from within North America.

The first cross-country trains inaugurated by CPR in 1886 were dubbed, fittingly, the *Pacific Express* (westbound) and *Atlantic Express* (eastbound). In his book *More Classic Trains*, Arthur Dubin describes their equipment: "The new cars were built with exteriors of varnished solid mahogany; interiors were satinwood, inlaid with brass and mother-of-pearl in Japanese designs. Parisian marble lavatories contained fittings of beaten bronze. Clerestory window ventilators were of colored Venetian glass; upholstery was sea-green plush; floors were covered with Turkey carpets." Total running time was almost 139 hours, for an average speed of less than 21 mph (34 kmh) on the 2,906-mile (4,688-kilometer) journey.

In 1899, CPR launched a new transcontinental train, the *Imperial Limited*, using cars whose appointments were, the railway said, "near perfection." The name, Lamb says,

"Notes by the Way" was Soo Line's guide to the route from Chicago to Vancouver and included extensive descriptions of CPR's resort properties in the Rockies. The cover depicts Banff Springs Hotel. *Author collection*

reflected "the conception of the Canadian Pacific as an all-Imperial British route to the Orient." This seasonal train initially operated on a schedule of just over 100 hours between Montreal and Vancouver, increasing the average speed to 29 mph (47 kmh), although in subsequent years its schedule was lengthened somewhat.

A June 1909 timetable shows Train 1, the *Imperial Limited*, departing Montreal at 10:10 a.m. The next day, the traveler arrived at Fort William at 8:30 p.m., having traveled the north shore of Lake Superior for much of the day. Arrival at Winnipeg was the next morning at 9:45 a.m. That afternoon and most of the next day were spent crossing the prairies, with arrival at Calgary at 5:20 p.m. The Great Divide between Alberta and British Columbia was reached just before

10:00 p.m.; the train's schedule denied westbound passengers the opportunity to see the Rockies and Selkirks in daylight. However, after a noon departure from Kamloops, four days after leaving Montreal, travelers were able to enjoy the scenic Thompson and Fraser river canyons before a 10:00 p.m. arrival in Vancouver.

Equipment on the *Imperial Limited* consisted of first-class coaches, standard sleepers, tourist sleepers, and colonist cars. The tourist sleepers were for the budget-minded traveler and were less luxuriously appointed than standard sleeping cars.

The colonist cars were a very Spartan type of conveyance aimed at the settler market. They were, quite literally, a hard class of service, lacking both upholstery and bedding (which the passenger was expected to supply). Dubin notes that "thousands of immigrants from Europe who arrived in Canada at the turn of the century spent their first nights in Canada aboard Colonist cars."

One variation from standard North American practice, introduced by Van Horne, was that CPR's sleepers and diners were operated by the railway itself, and not by the Pullman Company. This gave CPR control over the quality of service, which was paramount in its approach to the passenger business. Van Horne's former employer, the Milwaukee Road, followed a similar practice. Many CPR passenger cars were constructed at the company's Angus Shops in Montreal.

CPR recognized that if it wanted to fully exploit the potential of its western resorts, it had to serve not just Canada, but the U.S. market as well. Soo Line, with its route from Chicago to the West, was ideally

suited for this purpose, and in June 1900 a section of the *Imperial Limited* began operating via Moose Jaw, Saskatchewan, and the Soo–CPR interchange at Portal, North Dakota, with cars running through between Chicago and Vancouver.

The Soo Line also represented the eastern leg of a through service that CPR established between St. Paul and Portland, Oregon. From east to west, the complete route was:

- Soo Line from St. Paul to Portal, North Dakota;
- CPR from Portal, via Moose Jaw and Crowsnest Pass, to Kingsgate, British Columbia/Eastport, Idaho;
- CPR's Spokane International subsidiary from Eastport to Spokane; and
- Union Pacific affiliate Oregon Railway & Navigation from Spokane to Portland.

The *Imperial Limited* was eclipsed as CPR's premier passenger train by the *Trans-Canada Limited* in June 1919. That name had been used on summer-season trains as early as 1907, but the train introduced in 1919 represented a higher standard than any of its forebears. It carried only standard (i.e., first-class) sleepers, including a seven-compartment, one–drawing room car, and a three-compartment, one–drawing room observation car, plus a dining car between Montreal and Vancouver. A Toronto section connected at Sudbury.

Initially the train operated on a schedule of 93 hours and 30 minutes from Montreal to Vancouver, and 92 hours and 15 minutes in the opposite direction. By June 1925, an additional four hours had been cut out of the train's schedule, and the CPR timetable alerted passengers to "the convenient hours of arrival and departure at all major cities and resorts." In both directions, the spectacular

CPR train No. 8, the eastbound *Dominion*, is powered by Class T1a Selkirk 5906 as its passes Yoho, British Columbia, just out of the Lower Spiral Tunnel, in August 1938. *Photo by Otto Perry, Courtesy of Denver Public Library, Western History Collection/OP-20506*

The motor car was a low-cost solution to the need for passenger service on lightly used branch lines, and was a precursor of the Budd Rail Diesel Car. Here, CPR 9004 pauses at Guelph Junction, Ontario, in August 1957, while express is loaded. *Jim Shaughnessy*

segment between Banff and Revelstoke was traversed in daylight.

CPR's transcontinental service reached a new peak in 1931, with four passenger trains in each direction wending their way through the tunnels and mountain passes of western Canada:

- The all–sleeping car *Trans-Canada Limited*, between Montreal and Vancouver, with a connecting section to Toronto;
- The *Mountaineer*, an all-sleeper train between Chicago and Vancouver, operating via Soo Line east of Portal;
- The Montreal–Vancouver *Imperial*, carrying coaches and sleepers, including cars that connected at Moose Jaw with the *Soo-Pacific Express* to and from Chicago; and
- *The Dominion*, a Toronto–Vancouver coach and sleeper train that also handled a number of shorter-distance cars, including sleepers between Toronto and Winnipeg, Fort William and Winnipeg, Winnipeg and Calgary, Medicine Hat, Alberta, and Calgary, and Calgary and Vancouver.

The Dominion was the only one of these named trains to survive World War II, although the remnants of the *Imperial* lived on as unnamed Trains 1 and 2 between Montreal and Vancouver. There were, in fact, two *Dominions*: one between Vancouver and Montreal (Trains 7 and 8), the other serving Toronto (Trains 3 and 4). The latter had a U.S. connection at Moose Jaw, the *Soo-Dominion*, which operated via Soo Line between Portal and St. Paul, and Chicago & North Western between St. Paul and Chicago.

Passenger Service Reaches a Peak

The year 1944 represented an all-time peak in passengers carried by CPR: 18,461,000. For comparative purposes, passengers carried in other selected years were:

- 1886: 1,791,000 (the first year following completion of the transcontinental line)
- 1910: 11,173,000 (the first year that passenger volume exceeded 10 million)
- 1920: 16,925,000 (a record that held until 1944)
- 1933: 7,174,000 (the low point between the World Wars)

• 1940: 7,781,000 (less than half the volume that the railway would carry only four years later)

In any year, most passengers who rode CPR did so in coach. But by looking at those trains that carried first-class equipment (sleeping cars for overnight travel and parlor cars for day trips) during the peak year of 1944, it's possible to gain an appreciation for the changes that occurred over the next three decades, when all but a handful of the first-class services would be eliminated. All of the trains described below carried coaches as well.

In the East, CPR's November 1944 timetable shows two trains daily in each direction between Montreal and Saint John, New Brunswick: Trains 40 and 42 eastbound and 39 and 41 westbound, all of which carried sleepers. Trains 39 and 40 also had a buffet parlor car between Montreal and Megantic, Quebec (the point where the route crossed into Maine). Some cars on these trains operated through to Halifax via Canadian National (CPR's own route to Halifax required a ferry crossing, but the ferry did not carry railcars).

Another important overnight train serving Saint John was the *Gull*, which originated on CN in Halifax. CPR took the *Gull* from Saint John as far as the McAdam, New Brunswick/Vanceboro, Maine, border crossing, and it then ran on Maine Central to Portland and Boston & Maine to Boston.

CPR's Nova Scotia subsidiary, the Dominion Atlantic Railway, had its own first-class service in the form of a parlor car (as well as a diner) that ran between Halifax and Yarmouth, Nova Scotia, on Trains 95 and 98.

Between Montreal and Boston, on trains operated jointly by CPR and Boston & Maine (via their connection at Wells River, Vermont), travelers had a choice between the daytime *Alouette* (with a buffet parlor observation car) and the overnight *Red Wing*, which ran with a three-compartment, one–drawing

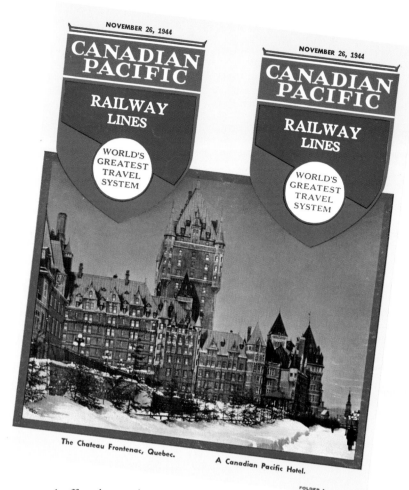

The Chateau Frontenac, Quebec.

A Canadian Pacific Hotel.

FOLDER A

room buffet observation car, as well as a twelve-section, two–double bedroom sleeper.

In the Quebec–Montreal–Ottawa–Toronto–Windsor corridor, where CPR and CN had pooled their passenger services since the early 1930s, there were a number of coach-only services, but also several trains that offered first-class service.

Trains 357 and 358 between Quebec and Montreal departed each day just before midnight, each with a sleeping car and coaches. Thanks to a slow schedule on the 178-mile (286-kilometer) route, they arrived at their destinations after 6:00 a.m., but sleeping car passengers could remain on board until 7:45 a.m. (Montreal) or 8:00 a.m. (Quebec City).

Four trains in each direction operated each day between Montreal and Toronto, two via CPR and two via CN. There were, in fact, two 11:00 p.m. departures from Montreal, one via each route. Both of these evening trains carried a heavy complement of sleeping cars on the

The November 1944 CPR timetable portrays the company's landmark Château Frontenac hotel at Quebec City. The contents of the timetable provide information on a cornucopia of rail passenger services. *Author collection*

Above: One of the last mixed trains to operate the CPR system was a Dominion Atlantic service between Windsor and Truro, Nova Scotia. Here, the train is shown at Windsor in May 1975. *Stan Smaill*

Right: In July 1962, CPR Dominion Atlantic Budd car 9059 loads passengers at Kentville, Nova Scotia, on its daily run from Halifax to Yarmouth, Nova Scotia, with a stop at Digby for the ferry connection across the Bay of Fundy to Saint John, New Brunswick. *Jim Shaughnessy*

route, which was just over 330 miles (531 kilometers) via either railway. The CPR edition, Train 21 (the *Chicago Express*) had sleepers for Toronto, Hamilton, London, and Detroit. They returned eastbound on Train 22, the *Overseas*, arriving each morning at 7:45 a.m. at CPR's Windsor Station, Montreal.

The other named trains on this route were the *Canadian* and the *Royal York*. There was some irony here, because the Royal York was CPR's huge hotel in Toronto, yet the train of this name operated westbound from CN's Montreal station and eastbound into CPR's. The *Canadian* ran westbound from the CPR

A Montreal-bound commuter train makes its way through an early-spring snowstorm, at Westmount, Quebec, in April 1975. *Phil Mason*

station, and eastbound into CN's. That name would be used, starting in 1955, by CPR's transcontinental train.

Sleepers also ran in this corridor between Ottawa and Toronto, Toronto and Detroit, and Toronto and Chicago (via New York Central's affiliate, Michigan Central, west of Detroit).

Toronto was also the endpoint for sleeper operations to several destinations in the north-eastern United States: Boston, New York, Pittsburgh, and Cleveland. Trains carrying these cars operated via CPR between Toronto and Hamilton, and then via the Toronto, Hamilton & Buffalo Railway, which served as CPR's link to several U.S. railroads at Buffalo, but primarily the New York Central system. TH&B was later absorbed by CPR.

Toronto, Hamilton & Buffalo was controlled by New York Central System and its affiliates, Michigan Central Railroad and Canada Southern Railway, which together owned 73 percent of its stock. CPR owned the remainder. In 1977, Canadian Pacific bought the former NYC-controlled shares from Penn Central, and subsequently integrated the TH&B into the CPR system. *Author collection*

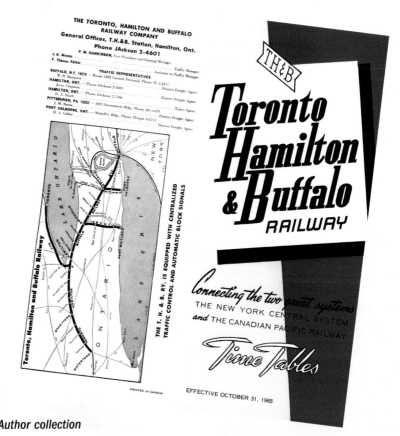

Another train that carried sleepers (as well as a café parlor car) was unnamed 27 and 28, between Toronto, Sudbury, and Sault Ste. Marie.

In the West, to reach St. Paul from Winnipeg, one could ride a sleeping car on the *Winnipeger*, which operated via the Soo Line south of the border at Emerson, Manitoba/Noyes, Minnesota. Soo Line also operated sleepers on its own routes between Chicago and both Duluth-Superior and Minneapolis–St. Paul.

Sleepers operated between Calgary and Edmonton, Alberta; Regina and Prince Albert, Saskatchewan; and Regina and Saskatoon, Saskatchewan.

Between Calgary and Vancouver the traveler who wanted to experience something different could enjoy a sleeper operating via Lethbridge, Alberta, and the Crowsnest Pass route, on trains 542/11 and 12/537. Train 11

Train 11, the *Kootenay Express*, seen here in May 1951, ran from Medicine Hat, Alberta, to Vancouver. The sleeper *Shaunavon* was a twelve-section, one–drawing room car, part of a group built in 1930 and 1931. Photographer Philip Hastings did not record the location of this photo, but it is believed to be on the Boundary Subdivision in southern British Columbia. *Photo by Philip Hastings, courtesy of California State Railroad Museum/negative no. 212*

Photographer Jim Shaughnessy's notes for this January 1955 photo read, "A -10° Fahrenheit breeze from the west blows steam around F9A 1416 as it waits to depart CPR's Montreal Windsor Station for Toronto." To the left is the dome of St. James Cathedral, renamed Mary Queen of the World Cathedral in 1955. At right is CPR's headquarters tower, part of Windsor Station. *Jim Shaughnessy*

(the *Kootenay Express*) covered the 962 miles (1,548 kilometers) between Medicine Hat, Alberta, and Vancouver, in approximately 41 hours, for an average speed of 23 mph (37 kmh). Its eastbound counterpart, Train 12 (the *Kettle Valley Express*) consumed just over 48 hours for the trip, with the longer time attributable to a layover of six hours at Nelson, British Columbia. These trains carried sleepers between Vancouver and both Penticton, British Columbia, and Lethbridge, as well as the Vancouver–Calgary sleeper. A café parlor car also operated between Penticton and Calgary.

Aside from these first-class services, CPR's November 1944 timetable showed coach-only trains on thousands of miles of trackage, both main and branch line. In addition, the timetable provided information about Canadian Pacific hotels and lodges; "express motor vehicle" routes in British Columbia; British Columbia coast steamship services; Canadian Pacific Air Lines schedules; and both transatlantic and transpacific steamship services. It was hard to refute CPR's claim to being the "World's Greatest Travel System."

Postwar Changes

Life changed for the railroads after World War II. The war effort had given a boost to the young airline industry, promoting technological improvements that were adapted in commercial aircraft and giving many Canadians their first taste of air travel (even if it was in an uncomfortable military transport plane). Automobile ownership increased and the trend toward suburban living made rail travel less practical.

CPR was not willing to concede the passenger travel market to other modes without a fight. It staked its claim to a share of that market on April 24, 1955, with the launching of the streamlined *Canadian*.

CPR's Web site (www.cpr.ca) describes the train as follows: "Two dome cars, a handsome dining car with excellent food, and a variety of sleeping arrangements: roomettes, double bedrooms, drawing rooms, berths and more. . . . The last car of each train . . . had a rounded-end observation lounge, a beverage room with the dome level above it, and first class sleeping space made up of a large drawing room and two bedrooms." The 173 cars, which had stainless-steel exteriors and were built by the Budd Company of Philadelphia, represented an investment of $40 million.

An advertisement by the Budd Company of Philadelphia, builder of the equipment for *The Canadian*, which made its debut in 1955. *Author collection*

When CPR launched *The Canadian* in 1955 there was enough equipment available to put some stainless-steel cars, including dome observations, on the now-secondary *Dominion*. Here, one of the Park-series cars prepares to depart Montreal on *The Dominion*, train No. 7. *Jim Shaughnessy*

The new train operated on a tighter schedule than any of its predecessors: 71 hours and 10 minutes from Montreal to Vancouver, and 50 minutes less eastbound. "Crump was hopeful," writes Lamb, "that with new equipment of the highest standard the transcontinental service could be both a prestige operation and a paying proposition for many years to come." According to those who knew him, Norris Crump would later consider his support for the new service to be one of the biggest blunders of his career, since it prolonged the railway's participation in a money-losing business.

But in the summer of 1955, the optimism of the time was reflected in the robust schedules of the railway's transcontinental service, which featured five distinct schedules west of Moose Jaw. Aside from *The Canadian*, they included *The Dominion*, the CPR-Soo *Mountaineer*, and two unnamed transcontinental trains in each direction.

Despite CPR's heavy investment in passenger equipment in the mid-1950s, financial losses mounted during the 1960s. Part of the reason can be seen in the company's declining passenger volumes:

9,529,000 in 1954; 7,059,000 in 1960; and 5,306,000 in 1970.

By 1966, all transcontinental trains except *The Canadian* had been discontinued (although *The Dominion* was briefly revived in 1967 in connection with Expo 67 in Montreal), and many other passenger trains had come to their end as well. In 1970, CPR announced that it wished to discontinue transcontinental passenger service completely. Predictably, the traveling public's reaction was negative, but even the Canadian Transportation Commission acknowledged that CPR was losing upwards of $15 million per year on the service.

This occurred at a time when the U.S. government's answer to money-losing rail passenger services, Amtrak, was in its formative stages. Canada would follow suit with its equiv-

It's July 1968, and *The Canadian*, CPR Train 1, sails west at track speed through Alfred, Ontario, en route to Ottawa on the M&O Subdivision, on the first leg of its transcontinental voyage from Montreal to Vancouver. *Bill Linley*

In early April 1970, a snow squall greets the passengers on westbound Train 1, *The Canadian*, at Medicine Hat, Alberta. On the right, Budd Rail Diesel Car 9022 waits to depart on Train 307 to Lethbridge, Alberta. The RDC, or "Dayliner" on CPR, was found in services throughout Canada, from Vancouver Island in the West to Nova Scotia in the East. *Steve Patterson*

CPR Dayliner 9058, operating as Dominion Atlantic Train 2 from Yarmouth to Halifax, crosses the Bear River in May 1975. *Stan Smaill*

In 1979, VIA Rail Canada took over operation of the Montreal–Saint John *Atlantic Limited* from CPR. Here, a holiday-lengthened Train 12, led by a former CN FPA-4, and carrying green flags to indicate a following section, makes a nocturnal stop for its crew change at Brownville Junction, Maine. *George Pitarys*

alent several years later. In the meantime, CPR continued to operate *The Canadian*, the Montreal–Saint John *Atlantic Limited* (which used equipment identical to that of *The Canadian*), and several secondary services, albeit with government subsidies helping to stem the red ink.

CN, at the time still a government-owned corporation with a more extensive (and therefore more draining) investment in passenger service than CPR, took the lead in extricating itself from the passenger service through the formation of a new entity, to be known as VIA. The change was at first more a matter of

The date is Sunday, July 25, 1965. According to photographer Bill Linley, "A gaggle of RDCs was a regular feature of quiet Sunday afternoons in the Ottawa Coach Yard adjacent to the Rideau Canal. These five cars will be filled to capacity by the time they arrive in Montreal from Ottawa this evening, after operating as Lachute Subdivision Train 134." In the background at left is the Château Laurier hotel, built by Grand Trunk Railway. *Bill Linley*

marketing and brand identity than a real solution to the passenger problem, but it soon evolved into a joint effort between both railways. In the fall of 1976, a VIA timetable was distributed listing both companies' passenger services.

With the model of government involvement in the passenger business already well established in the United States, Canada soon followed suit with the 1978 formation of a crown corporation, VIA Rail Canada. It took over operation and financial responsibility for the country's intercity passenger trains.

The Canadian lived on as the name of VIA Rail's transcontinental train, even though it operated over CN trackage. Its splendid stainless-steel Budd equipment was still operating in the twenty-first century, more than 50 years after it was delivered, with a new generation of passengers enjoying the view from its *Park* series observation dome cars.

In August 1969, Budd-built Rail Diesel Car 9111 is ready to depart Megantic, Quebec, en route to Montreal as Train 201. *Bill Linley*

In the mid-1980s, CPR's U.S. affiliate, Soo Line Railroad, negotiated an agreement with CSX that allowed Soo trains to operate via CSX between Chicago and Detroit. This eliminated a circuitous Soo Line–CPR routing via Sault Ste. Marie, Michigan, and Sudbury, Ontario. The main beneficiary of the shorter route was container traffic, as shown on this westbound train at Newtonville, Ontario, in October 1986, en route to Chicago via Windsor and Detroit. In 2005, several of CPR's Chicago–Detroit trains were shifted to a Norfolk Southern routing. The blue containers belong to Cast North America, which was a longtime CPR customer and a CP Ships competitor in the North Atlantic. In 1995, Canadian Pacific purchased Cast and merged it into CP Ships. *Eric Blasko*

CHAPTER SIX

CANADIAN PACIFIC BULKS UP, THEN SLIMS DOWN: *1972–1996*

The company that Norris "Buck" Crump left to his successors in 1972 was far more diverse than it had been when he moved into the president's office 17 years earlier. The railway generated just over 50 percent more in earnings in 1972 than it had in 1955, but the company as a whole was producing more than twice as much net income. The difference? Oil and gas, timberlands, real estate, and other non-rail operations were a more important part of the company in 1972, and were, for the most part, very profitable ventures.

One-of-a-kind RSD17 CP 8921 was built by MLW as a demonstrator in 1957 and saw service on Pacific Great Eastern and Canadian National before it was acquired by CPR in 1959. It spent much of its CPR career based at CPR's Toronto Yard in Agincourt, Ontario, and was known locally as the "Empress of Agincourt." In October 1993, it is on the head end of Montreal–Windsor automotive Train 919, crossing the Mud Lake Bridge west of Perth, Ontario, on the Belleville Subdivision.
John Leopard

But CP Limited was not at the end of its diversification phase; it was actually at the start of it. Over the next several years, the company added a diverse array of companies to the CP Investments portfolio, including Algoma Steel (1974), Great Lakes Forest Products (1974), Baker Commodities (1976), Syracuse China (1978), Maple Leaf Mills (1980), and Canadian International Paper (1981).

Much of this acquisition activity was accomplished through the efforts of Crump's successor (first as president of the company from 1966 to 1972, and then as chairman from 1972 to 1981), Ian D. Sinclair. The diversification of Canadian Pacific had started almost 90 years before, under George Stephen's leadership, when he and William Van Horne set up enterprises connected to the railway—steamships, hotels, communications—and continued as the company made the most of assets it acquired through the operation of the railway. In the 1970s, however, acquisitions were motivated purely by financial goals, not by how well they could produce traffic for the railway.

Sinclair prided himself on being a businessman, not a railwayman. The railway, Sinclair believed, was an inherently cyclical business; it was too dependent, he felt, on commodities like grain, timber, and steel that could be up one year and down the next. His emphasis on diversification was timely—the 1970s were a tough time to make money in the railway business.

But as with many business trends, the cycle soon started going the other way, not just at Canadian Pacific but at other North American railways, which began to adopt a new business mantra: "Stick to your knitting." CP Limited shareholders faced the unwelcome news that not all of their non-rail investments were consistent moneymakers.

In 1981, Sinclair relinquished the positions of chairman and CEO of CP Limited to Fred Burbidge, and the board of directors picked William Stinson to succeed him as president. In 1986, Stinson became CEO and R. W. Campbell succeeded Burbidge as chairman.

David Cruise and Alison Griffiths note that this change "signaled a return to the CP tradition of making the president the real power in the company," as well as a sea change in the company's business portfolio: "In a flurry of activity, matched only by Sinclair's acquisition spree of the seventies, Stinson hacked away at the company. Gone were a host of subsidiaries:

After the CP sold the Dominion Atlantic Railway in Nova Scotia, it transferred the SW1200RS units that had been the mainstay of the DAR for many years to McAdam, New Brunswick. In October 1994 a trio of them is seen in front of McAdam's impressive station. *George Pitarys*

MLW C424 4222 leads Train 281 past milepost 19 in Maine's very remote Moosehead Subdivision. Only a mile to the west is the site of Maine's worst railway disaster, a head-on collision in December 1919 in which 19 passengers and 4 crewmen lost their lives. This line is today operated by the Montreal, Maine & Atlantic Railway. *George Pitarys*

the flight kitchens; Château Insurance; Maple Leaf Mills; Express Airborne (a division of CP Trucks); an office building in London; several assets controlled by AMCA, an equipment-manufacturing firm; and Steep Rock Resources Inc." In 1986, CP Limited's 52.46 percent interest in Cominco was sold to Teck Corporation, and the following year CP Air was sold to Pacific Western Airlines. Syracuse China was sold in 1989.

Maine's largest lake, Moosehead, gave its name to the CPR subdivision between Brownville Junction, Maine, and Megantic, Quebec. Here, it provides a beautiful backdrop from the high rock cut locally known as Bald Bluff, west of Greenville, Maine. In July 1992, a pair of RS18 units snakes Train 281 along the desolate west shore of the lake. *George Pitarys*

However, Stinson was a pragmatist on the subject of diversification, not an ideologue. In 1988, the company sold its 53.8 percent interest in Algoma Steel, but acquired school bus operator and waste management company Laidlaw Transportation Limited. The same year, it bought out CN's interest in CNCP Telecommunications, as well as CN's nine-property hotel chain.

As it entered the 1990s, Canadian Pacific was, by any definition, still a conglomerate, even if it wasn't as diverse as it had been a decade earlier. The company's business portfolio included rail, shipping, and trucking services, petroleum, coal, forest products, hotels, real estate, telecommunications, industrial and construction services, and waste services. Some of these subsidiaries would fall by the wayside in the early 1990s, but CP Limited would remain a diverse enterprise for the next decade.

Grain Transport:
Toward a More Rational System

CPR had agreed in 1897 to reduce its rates on grain from specific prairie origins to Port Arthur and Fort William, in return for a federal subsidy in connection with the line being built through Crows Nest Pass and into the interior of southern British Columbia. Over time, the Crow Rate structure was expanded to apply to Canadian National, as well as CPR; to cover all grain origins, as well as certain types of grain not included in the original agreement; and to include westward shipments of grain to Vancouver. Most

It's minus 11 degrees Fahrenheit as Train 281 races by one of the most dominating features in Quebec's eastern townships, Mount Orford, in February 1993. Mount Orford is 23 miles (37 kilometers) west of Sherbrooke, Quebec, on the line to Montreal. This segment is now part of Montreal, Maine & Atlantic. *George Pitarys*

significantly, in 1925 the Crow Rates were enacted into law and were thereafter considered "statutory rates." There was no escalation mechanism built into them; they remained fixed regardless of inflation.

Although larger cars, longer trains, and other operating efficiencies helped offset increases in wages and other operating expenses, the net effect of more than a half-century of inflation was to eliminate the railways' profit from the transportation of grain and, therefore, their incentive to invest in the grain transportation system. In 1974, a consultant was appointed by the government to analyze the cost of moving grain and determine which parties were bearing that cost. He determined that 38 percent of the cost was being paid by farmers through the rail rates they paid, 24 percent was being borne by the federal government through subsidies, and 38 percent was being absorbed by the railways.

Although a series of investigations in the 1960s and 1970s all reached a similar conclusion—that the Crow rates were too low to support railway investment in the grain net-

Grain is an important contributor to CPR's revenue base. Here, a covered hopper is loaded at Tompkins, Saskatchewan, in October 1989. *Phil Mason*

The Vancouver waterfront has long featured a rich variety of transportation operations. The dining car York is ready to depart as part of the Montreal-bound *Canadian* in September 1971. In the background a CPR switch engine handles freight for some of the waterfront area's many industries. Farther in the background is the *Indian Mail*, a 605-foot (185-meter) cargo liner operated by American Mail Lines. *Photo by Philip Hastings, courtesy of California State Railroad Museum/negative no. 2439CPR*

In this May 1982 view of CPR's waterfront yard in Vancouver, the former CP steamship *Princess Patricia* can be seen on the right. The *Princess Patricia* was launched in 1948 and entered service the following year between Vancouver, Victoria, and Seattle. It later saw service between Vancouver and Alaska before being retired in 1981. *Phil Mason*

Beginning with the advent of unit coal trains in 1970, and continuing with the growth in coal, grain, sulfur, and container traffic, CPR has engaged in one project after another designed to allow it to run more and longer trains west of Calgary. One such project was a grade reduction west of Revelstoke, British Columbia, between mileposts 70 and 80 on the Shuswap Subdivision. This grade, Notch Hill, at 1.8 percent, was the last significant obstacle encountered by westbound tonnage trains destined for Vancouver. In 1978, CPR constructed a new 11-mile (18-kilometer) track between Tappen and Notch Hill, with a 2-mile loop that allowed the ruling grade to be reduced to 1.0 percent. Here, in July 1984, a westbound grain train traverses the loop track. *Phil Mason*

work—only limited measures were taken to address the problem. Primarily, those measures consisted of government subsidies to the railways and government purchase of covered hopper cars for the grain business (by 1981, the federal government had bought 10,000 such cars).

Closely related to the grain rate question was the issue of branch line abandonments, which were difficult for the railways to implement under prevailing regulations. The tide turned following the release of the Hall Commission report in 1977, which recommended that CPR and CN be allowed to abandon 2,165 miles (3,484 kilometers) of prairie branches over a four-year period. This set the stage for eventual abandonment of many light-density lines.

As for rates, relief came for CPR and CN in 1983 with the passage of the Western Grain Transportation Act (WGTA). It provided for a new grain rate structure, effective on January 1, 1984, and subject to annual review. Grain rates would be based on the railways' operating costs, but capped at 10 percent of the world price of grain. Theoretically, at least, the grain business would now be profitable for the railways. Although CPR is never eager to publicize its profit margin on specific lines of business, its words and actions concerning the grain business since 1984 indicate that it does, indeed, view the business as profitable.

Part of the Mount Macdonald project was a 4,032-foot (1,229-meter) viaduct that allowed the eastern approach to be constructed on a 40-degree slope while minimizing environmental impacts. In October 1989, Train 471 comes off the viaduct, which was named after CPR chief engineer John Fox. *Steve Patterson*

An Increasing Focus on the West

By the 1970s, the CPR was increasingly focused on the West. The watershed event was the beginning of unit-train coal movements to Vancouver for export in 1970; other commodities soon became part of that export flow, notably potash and sulfur. With the passage of the Western Grain Transportation Act, unit grain trains moving toward Vancouver also became a welcome sight in the eyes of CPR management.

The growth in western traffic prompted CPR to look at its Calgary–Vancouver main line and ask how it could move more business over the mountainous territory. Largely single-track, it posed several obstacles to be dealt with, three of which were completed between 1977 and 1981:

- The 1.7 percent grade on the Shuswap Subdivision immediately west of Revelstoke

As a westbound train travels over the Macdonald track it first encounters the 1.2-mile (1.9-kilometer) Mount Shaughnessy Tunnel. In October 1989, a westbound train behind SD40-2 5813 emerges from the Mount Shaughnessy bore and will soon enter the longer Mount Macdonald tunnel. Steve Patterson

to Clanwilliam. A 4.5-mile (7.2-kilometer) westbound track, separate from the original route, was constructed starting in June 1977.
- The 1.8 percent grade over Notch Hill, also on the Shuswap Subdivision. To reduce the grade, an 11-mile (18-kilometer) westbound track was constructed, incorporating a horseshoe-type loop. Construction began in late 1977. Both Shuswap Subdivision projects were completed in December 1979.
- The 1.8 percent grade from Lake Louise to the Continental Divide (known locally as the Great Divide) at Stephen, British

Westbound Train 481, operating as Extra 5912 West, emerges from the Mount Macdonald tunnel at Ross Peak, British Columbia, in October 1989. The tunnel is 9.1 miles (14.6 kilometers) in length and was placed into service on December 12, 1988. It eased the ruling westbound grade from 2.2 percent to 1 percent. The new tunnel passes 298 feet (91 meters) below the 1916 Connaught Tunnel, which remains in service and is used mainly by eastbound trains. *Steve Patterson*

Columbia, on the Laggan Subdivision. A 5.5-mile (8.9-kilometer) westbound track was constructed between September 1978 and May 1981.

At each of these locations, the westbound grade was reduced to approximately 1 percent. The completion of these projects left one major physical barrier to westbound tonnage trains: the long westward climb from Golden to the Connaught Tunnel in Rogers Pass. In 1981, CPR announced it would undertake a grade-reduction project in Rogers Pass by building a new tunnel under Mount Macdonald, at an ele-

vation 298 feet (91 meters) lower than the Connaught Tunnel. It would do so, however, only if a solution could be found to the economic loss that CPR sustained on the movement of export grain. That solution came in the form of the Western Grain Transportation Act.

The same year that the WGTA went into effect, 1984, CPR began work on the Rogers Pass project, CPR's most ambitious engineering project since the completion of the Spiral Tunnels and the Connaught Tunnel before World War I. In December 1988, the first revenue train operated through the new Mount Shaughnessy and Mount Macdonald tunnels.

The increasing volume of western business only served to accentuate the fact that CPR was really two railroads: bulk commodities west of Thunder Bay (formerly Port Arthur and Fort William) and manufactured products east of that point. The contrast was stark enough that CPR began to worry about how, or even whether, it could make money in the East.

In 1987, CPR divided its rail operations into two business units: one to focus on heavy haul freight and the other to develop intermodal freight systems. "This realignment," the company explained, "allows a more flexible response to market opportunities and competitive pressures resulting from regulatory reforms and changing business patterns in Canada and internationally." The names "heavy haul" and "intermodal" were, in a sense, euphemisms for the western and eastern parts of the CPR network.

Besides bulk business, the other source of growth in the West was international container traffic, largely consisting of imports from Asia destined to North American markets. In the 1980s, double-stack technology changed the economics of this business, but CPR's tunnels had to be modified to handle the higher-dimension loads. In 1993, it completed an 18-month project to enlarge 48 of its tunnels.

A Soo Line SD60 and SD40-2 power eastbound Train 204 at Donehower, Minnesota, in October 1995. This route was once Milwaukee Road's Chicago–Milwaukee–Twin Cities corridor, and at that time was mainly double-track with automatic block signals. Soo Line acquired the assets of the Milwaukee Road in 1985. In the late 1980s, Soo converted the route to single-track operation with centralized traffic control and 2.5-mile (4-kilometer) passing sidings approximately every 10 miles (16 kilometers). *John Leopard*

As the 1980s drew to a close, CPR became more deeply involved in the United States. The three midwestern roads in which CPR owned stock—Minneapolis, St. Paul & Sault Ste. Marie; Duluth, South Shore & Atlantic; and Wisconsin Central—had merged on January 1, 1961, to form Soo Line Railroad Company. CPR held approximately 56 percent of Soo Line's stock, and the two roads interchanged large volumes of traffic, but they were managed independently of each other. In 1985, Minneapolis-based Soo Line acquired the assets of the bankrupt Milwaukee Road.

In February 1991, units 4101-4302-4200 are on Soo Line's Humboldt transfer on the Mississippi River Bridge at Camden Place, Minneapolis. GP15C 4101 and GP30C 4302 had been recently repowered with Caterpillar diesel prime movers; all of the Caterpillar-powered units were off the roster by 1999. GP9 4200 was a former New York Central unit rebuilt by CPR in Montreal, retaining its EMD engine. Soo Line's candy-apple-red paint scheme was developed in 1989, replacing the railroad's previous livery of red, black, and light grey. *John Leopard*

The next few years were difficult ones for Soo Line as it digested the Milwaukee Road. The company shed much of its legacy trackage, primarily in Wisconsin, and moved its Minneapolis–Chicago traffic to the former Milwaukee Road main line. CPR attempted to sell its interest in Soo Line, but then reversed course and in 1990 acquired full ownership of Soo Line. In 1991, CPR began to eliminate the Soo Line identity, integrating the U.S. operations into its Canadian organization.

CPR took another step toward greater involvement in the U.S. with its 1991 purchase of the Delaware & Hudson Railway. The D&H had once billed itself as "The Bridge Line to New England and Canada"; its routes ran across New York State from west to east, and on a north-south axis from the Canadian border, just south of Montreal, to Albany and, via trackage rights, to the New York metropolitan area (Oak Island, New Jersey), Philadelphia, and all the way to Potomac Yard, Virginia. CPR would spend the next 15 years trying to make D&H profitable.

CPR Cuts Back in the East

In eastern Canada, CPR was ready to either radically remake the rail map or call it quits. Decades of erosion in the volume and profitability of eastern business had taken their toll. In 1988, the company carved out the portion of its network east of Megantic, Quebec, as a separate entity called Canadian Atlantic Railway. Giving the Maine and Maritime operations a separate identity did not, however, change their basic economics.

Early in 1993, the company announced: "Thousands of miles of uneconomic trackage must be shed in Canada. . . . After sustaining losses of $52 million in the last three years, CP Rail System announced it would seek regulatory approval to abandon all operations east of Sherbrooke, Quebec, a total of about 400 miles (645 kilometers) of track. . . . CP Rail System is also involved

in ongoing discussions with CN North America to rationalize railway facilities in Eastern Canada."

The talks with CN would drag on but ultimately lead nowhere. Government opposition to a rail monopoly in eastern Canada killed whatever chance might have existed for the two carriers to combine their systems east of Montreal. Elsewhere, CPR and CN did have more success in sharing facilities, such as between Montreal and North Bay, Ontario, where they agreed to a shared-track arrangement. Over the next decade they would find opportunities throughout Canada and the northeastern United States to cooperate operationally while competing commercially.

Between 1994 and 1996, CPR shed many eastern lines it considered uneconomic. Most were transferred to short-line operators whose more favorable cost structures and more focused local managements gave them an opportunity to compete where CPR had failed. Some of the milestones included:

•   In 1994, the former Dominion Atlantic Railway in Nova Scotia began operation as the Windsor & Hantsport Railway.

Train 80, a Farnham, Quebec–Newport, Vermont, turn job, rolls into the small Vermont village of North Troy, 14 miles (22 kilometers) short of its turnaround point, behind RS-18 8775 in February 1981. Like the east–west line across southern Quebec and western Maine, the segment from Farnham to Newport is now operated by Montreal, Maine & Atlantic. *George Pitarys*

Beginning in 1980, and continuing for the rest of the 1980s, CPR rebuilt RS-18s into RS-18us, with emphasis on upgrading the units' wiring, electrical systems, and cabs, as well as cutting down their short hoods for improved visibility. By the end of 1989, 69 of the MLW products had been rebuilt at Angus Shops in Montreal. Three graduates of the program, CP 1800-1842-1804, power the CPR wayfreight from Newport, Vermont, to Farnham, Quebec, as it performs switching at Richford, Vermont, in February 1988. *Jim Shaughnessy*

CPR had a fleet of 44 MLW M-636 locomotives. The units, built in 1969 and 1970, were troublesome, but most of them remained in service until the early 1990s. Here, M-636 4708 leads Train 522 through Bury, Quebec, in April 1981. *Stan Smaill*

Extra 8470 north almost appears to be at sea as it crosses the windswept plains south of St. Pie, Quebec, on the St. Guillaume Subdivision, in February 1976. Mount Yamaska looms in the distance. A large feed mill in Ste. Rosalie is the train's destination. *George Pitarys*

- In 1995, the New Brunswick Southern Railway began operating over former CPR trackage from McAdam to Saint John, New Brunswick.
- In 1996, privately owned Iron Road Railways inaugurated service under the Quebec Southern Railway name on several Quebec lines: Lennoxville–St. Jean; Brookport–Wells River, Vermont; Farnham–Ste. Rosalie Junction; and Farnham–Stanbridge. The same year, short-line RaiLink–Ottawa Valley took over former CPR lines between Cartier and Smiths Falls, Ontario, and between Mattawa and Temiskaming, Quebec.
- In 1997, Huron Central Railway became the operator of the Sault Ste. Marie –Sudbury, Ontario, line. Also in 1997, Quebec Gatineau Railway took over two CPR subdivisions between Quebec City and Hull, Quebec.

Additional short-line conversions followed over the next several years, but by 1998 CPR's operations in eastern Canada had been radically trimmed.

CP 4555, an M-630 produced by MLW in 1970, is southbound on Train 908 at LaSalle, Quebec, in May 1985. Like the M-636, the M-630 had high maintenance costs and a poor reputation for reliability. Nevertheless, CPR kept its fleet of six-axle MLW units in service for more than 20 years, as it was faced with steadily increasing traffic and a shortage of funds to invest in new power. *Stan Smaill*

Eastbound Train 522 passes through Cookshire, Quebec, in February 1982, with a set of three six-axle MLW units for power, led by M-630 4550. *Stan Smaill*

Near Parson, British Columbia, on the Windermere Subdivision, in September 1999, CP 3135 and two other GP38-2 units power the Golden wayfreight. This line is used mainly by coal trains from mines in southeastern British Columbia. *John Leopard*

CHAPTER SEVEN

UNWINDING THIRTY YEARS OF DIVERSIFICATION: *1996–2006*

Early in 1995, Canadian Pacific Limited recorded two executive

changes in the annual report sent to shareholders: "David O'Brien

joined Canadian Pacific Limited as president and chief operating offi-

cer in February 1995 following a highly-successful tenure as chief exec-

utive officer of PanCanadian Petroleum. . . . In March 1995, Rob

Ritchie was appointed chief executive officer of CP Rail System."

A 1996 financial restructuring gave Canadian Pacific Railway a

new legal identity as a wholly owned subsidiary of the parent company,

General Electric AC4400CW 9679 leads eastbound Train 470 at Ernfold, Saskatchewan, in September 1998. Photographer John Leopard notes that, "Nearly 6,000 wood grain elevators stood above the Canadian prairies in the 1930s; now there are fewer than 1,000. Construction of massive concrete grain-handling facilities capable of loading 100-plus car unit trains was responsible for this drop in numbers. For every new facility built, 8 to 15 wooden elevators were demolished." *John Leopard*

rather than as a division. That might seem like a matter of semantics, but it allowed CPR to deal with the capital markets separately from CP Limited. It was also a way of telling CPR management that from this point forward, the railway's survival was up to them. There would be no more cross-subsidies from CPL's more profitable businesses.

William Stinson retired in May 1996 after ten years as chief executive officer of Canadian Pacific. A key decision made during the final months of his tenure was to move the

headquarters of both CP Limited and the railway from Montreal to Calgary.

O'Brien was now chairman, president, and CEO. Over the next five years, he would preside over a dramatic remaking of Canadian Pacific. But first, there was some housekeeping to be done. Prior to O'Brien's arrival, the company had exited the trucking business and shed its remaining interest in Unitel, the successor to CNCP Telecommunications. In late 1996, it sold Marathon Realty. The following year, it sold its 18 percent interest in Laidlaw Inc. Its business portfolio now included CP Rail System, CP Ships, PanCanadian Petroleum (87 percent ownership), Fording Coal, and Canadian Pacific Hotels & Resorts Inc.

O'Brien's moves prompted the investment community to ask, "What is he up to?" In the three decades since Buck Crump and Ian Sinclair led Canadian Pacific down the

CPR Train 268 from Saratoga Springs to Albany, New York, passes the large GE Chemicals plant at Waterford, New York, on the former Delaware & Hudson, in May 1999. *Jim Shaughnessy*

path of diversification, there had been a change in style among large corporations. Conglomerates were no longer in favor. Investment returns from diversified companies had been disappointing and shareholders often blamed their managements for not being focused enough. In addition, conglomerates were not easy to understand, even for financial analysts, who tended to specialize in certain industries. Most of the analysts who followed Canadian Pacific were experts in transportation, so they didn't necessarily know what questions to ask about CPL's petroleum, coal, or hotel businesses.

O'Brien was cagey about his plans. He acknowledged that CPR might be a player in future North American rail mergers. He suggested that CPL might downplay its exposure to the commodity business, which could indicate a possible sale of the Fording Coal unit.

As late as November 2000, he still wasn't showing his hand. In a press briefing, he said, "We're obviously not going to build five global businesses. But we think we can build a couple of global businesses."

Streamlining the Railway

Although CPR's elimination of light-density lines from the network was well underway by the time that the corporate restructuring was announced in 1995, the railway was still not pleased with the performance of its eastern network.

When it announced that it would move its corporate headquarters to Calgary, CPR explained, "Montreal will be home to a new

147

eastern operating unit that will be run as a separate operation with a management team dedicated to achieving a regional railway cost structure. Its mandate will be to restore a money-losing operation to profitability. Key challenges include excess capacity and surplus network infrastructure, uncompetitive labour costs, modal competition from trucking, and the achievement of equitable treatment in fuel and property taxation policies." The eastern unit would be responsible "for transforming the railway's operations between Montreal, Toronto, Chicago and the U.S. northeast into the most efficient provider of transportation services in the region." Translation: for the right price, our eastern lines are for sale.

The next year, the eastern operation was given the name St. Lawrence & Hudson Railway Company Limited. Locomotives appeared in a modified paint scheme with the StL&H initials, and maps began to appear showing StL&H as the operator of the Chicago–Detroit–Toronto–Montreal main line, as well as the route to Buffalo and the entire D&H.

The network simplification plan already underway in the East was expanded to include portions of the former Soo Line. By

After absorbing Soo Line in 1990, and purchasing Delaware & Hudson in 1991, CPR changed its identity from CP Rail to CP Rail System. It also began using an international logo on its motive power, showing the flags of both Canada and the United States. Wearing the dual-flag scheme, CP SD40-2 5421 leads Train 271 at Central Bridge, New York, in May 2000. *Pat Yough*

the end of 1996, the company said it "had negotiated or was in the process of negotiating the sale, lease, discontinuance or shortlining of approximately 2,700 miles (4,350 kilometers) of line in Quebec, Ontario, Vermont and the U.S. midwest. The agreements cover 1,143 (1,840 kilometers) miles of line between Kansas City and Chicago, and in Iowa and Minnesota; 383 miles (616 kilometers) of branch lines in North Dakota; 240 miles (386 kilometers) in Quebec and Vermont; and 342 miles (550 kilometers) in Ontario between Smiths Falls and Coniston."

It didn't take CPR long to consummate a sale of the most attractive part of this package. In 1997, it sold the ex–Soo Line (originally

CPR was granted access to the New York City and Long Island markets as a condition of the Conrail breakup in 1999. This allowed New York City and Long Island shippers an alternative to CSX, which operates this part of the former Conrail system. In July 2002, CPR Train 505 (operating between Fresh Pond Yard in Queens and the former D&H yard in Saratoga Springs, New York) rolls north along the Harlem River on the Oak Point Link, built for freight trains to bypass the busy Mott Haven Junction, with SD40-2s 5698–5677. The lead unit wears the CPR logo introduced in 1997, which, in the company's words, "returns the beaver to its lofty position atop a shield with maple leaf motif, encircled by a band that incorporates the Canadian Pacific Railway name and the year 1881." *Pat Yough*

Two GP38-2 units, CP 3118 and 3039, power the westbound Assiniboia Tramp on the Wood Mountain Subdivision in September 1997. This Saskatchewan line was built at a time when the Canadian rail system was in expansion mode in order to open up new areas for agriculture. It was built in 1929 and reached as far west as Mankota. The summer of 1998 saw the last train service by CPR. Efforts to revive the 64-mile (103-kilometer) line as a short line failed, and in October 1999, the rail was removed. *John Leopard*

Milwaukee Road) route between Kansas City and Chicago, as well as the ex-Milwaukee "Corn Lines" in northern Iowa and southern Minnesota, for $380 million. The new operator was I&M Rail Link, an affiliate of Montana Rail Link, owned by Montana entrepreneur and construction magnate Dennis Washington. Within a few years, however, Washington's financial empire came under pressure; in 2002 the operation was sold to Iowa, Chicago

& Eastern Railroad, an affiliate of the Dakota, Minnesota & Eastern Railroad.

If CPR's commitment to retaining its Montreal–Toronto–Detroit–Chicago route seemed questionable when that line was thrown into StL&H, the company aimed to reverse that impression in 1997 when it announced that it would "likely retain [the line] as an integral part of its network." It was by no means an ironclad guarantee, but it

meant that the "for sale" sign implied by the formation of StL&H now referred largely to the former D&H.

In 1997, CPR made a symbolic return to its roots when it adopted the name "Canadian Pacific Railway" for public use (in lieu of CP Rail System). In 1997, it restored the beaver and shield to its corporate logo.

That same year, CPR began to revitalize its motive power fleet with AC-traction

Following CPR's acquisition of Delaware & Hudson in 1991, and particularly following the breakup of Conrail in 1999, CPR developed a close working relationship with Norfolk Southern, which utilized the former D&H routes to reach New England and eastern Canada. Symbolizing the transition, locomotives of each of the three roads line up at Kenwood Yard in Albany, New York, in June 1998. *Jim Shaughnessy*

locomotives. AC locomotives are widely thought to be better suited for heavy-duty and mountain operations than conventional DC units. In early 1998, CPR reported that in addition to 90 AC locomotives acquired the previous year, it would buy 91 such units in 1998 and another 81 in 1999, for a total of 262. By mid-2005, CPR's ownership of AC locomotives stood at 503.

By the end of 1998, the company had sold or abandoned 3,850 route miles (6,196 kilometers) over a three-year period, or about 70 percent of the 5,500 miles (8,850 kilometers)

identified as "non-core." As CPR shed unprofitable lines and worked to improve the efficiency of its core network, its operating ratio began to fall, reaching 79.2 in 1998, an improvement of more than 10 percentage points since 1994 when the operating ratio had stood at 89.4.

With the route map stabilized and with new assets in place to support more efficient operations, CPR implemented a new operating plan in 1999 aimed at "making the assets sweat," as Rob Ritchie often said. Key elements of the new plan included longer, heavier trains, as long as 9,000 feet (2,740 meters) in some corridors, up from a previous maximum of 7,200 feet (2,190 meters); fewer intermediate handlings at yard and terminals; and reductions in handling times at yards.

By the end of 2000, CPR had shaved another couple of points off its operating ratio

In October 1997, CP SD40-2 5798 leads an eastbound train past a Manitoba Pool elevator and a CPR water tank at Binscarth, Manitoba, on the Bredenbury Subdivision. This segment is part of the secondary main line between Portage la Prairie, Manitoba, and Wetaskiwin, Alberta (between Calgary and Edmonton), via Saskatoon, Saskatchewan. The line was completed in 1908 as a through route to improve CPR's competitive position versus Canadian Northern and Grand Trunk Pacific. *John Leopard*

since 1998 for an average of 76.9 on the year. Its system route mileage stood at 13,959 (22,465 kilometers), down from 18,100 (29,130 kilometers) in 1994. The railway generated 110 billion revenue ton-miles in 2000, up from 102 billion in 1994. And its workforce had shrunk, from 23,600 in 1994 to 17,519 in 2000.

2001: The Spinoff

Although O'Brien had promised for years to "narrow the focus" of the company, and said as recently as January 2001 that the conglomerate discount on CP's share price "cried for action," the company still took many observers by surprise with its announcement on February 13, 2001, that it planned to separate into five independent, publicly traded companies:

- Canadian Pacific Railway;

- CP Ships, by then the seventh-largest container shipping company in the world;
- PanCanadian Petroleum (86 percent owned by CPL), whose primary business was production and marketing of crude oil and natural gas;
- Fording Coal, Canada's largest coal producer; and
- Canadian Pacific Hotels, which controlled the Fairmont chain of luxury hotels, as well as the Delta chain in Canada.

Legally, the first four companies were spun off from the parent, which retained the hotel business and renamed itself Fairmont Hotels & Resorts Inc.

The spinoff was scheduled for October 1, 2001. Although turbulence in the financial markets following the terrorist attacks of

September 11 caused some to speculate that the spinoff might be deferred, it was not. Shareholders in CP Limited received shares in the five new operating companies, each of which was now free to chart its own course for the future.

A westbound freight, led by CP 5773, traverses the steep grades encountered in the valley of the Assiniboine River near Harrowby, Manitoba, on CPR's Bredenbury Subdivision in September 1996. Photographer John Leopard observes, "the Canadian prairies are far from flat: many valleys, lakes, and rivers are remnants of the glacial period that shaped the region's geography." *John Leopard*

Once Again, a Railway

The early years following CPR's rebirth as a pure rail company were full of challenges. Financially, it started life with a relatively heavy debt load, a parting gift from CP Limited, which had sought to spread its own debt among the operating companies in a way that was "appropriate" for their industries. Early on, there was optimism that the company's debt could be paid down as additional operating efficiencies helped improve its free cash flow, but that optimism didn't take into account the head-

winds that the company would face between 2001 and 2005.

First, there was drought. In 2002, the first full year of its operation as in independent company, CPR was faced with a grain crop that CEO Rob Ritchie described as "one of the smallest ever to come off the Canadian prairies." To compound the revenue shortfall, coal traffic was down, thanks to the ever-shifting dynamics of the world coal market.

Then there was the strong Canadian dollar, which did this Canadian company no

The Crowsnest Pass line west of Lethbridge, Alberta, had steep grades and many curves. In 1904, surveys began on a new line that, it was found, could be constructed with a ruling grade of 0.4 percent and eliminate 37 curves. The main obstruction was the Belly (later Oldman) River, which CPR bridged with a mile-long, 300-foot-high (91-meter) bridge. The bridge was completed in June 1909 and opened to traffic four months later. This is a loaded grain train en route to the Union Pacific interchange at Kingsgate in September 1998. *John Leopard*

favors. As U.S. revenues were translated into Canadian currency, the fluctuation in exchange rates meant lower revenues for CPR.

Third among the challenges of this period was the rise in the price of diesel fuel. In 2003, CPR spent $393 million on fuel. The next year, fuel expenses increased to $440 million. Further increases were to come: in the second quarter of 2005, the company was paying 47 percent more per gallon of diesel fuel than it had a year earlier. Fortunately for

its bottom line, CPR (like most other North American railroads) was able to pass a substantial percentage of the cost increase to its customers.

If there were headwinds, there were also factors that worked in favor of CPR, primarily the strength of its overall business. In 2001, the company generated 211 billion gross ton-miles of freight. By 2004, that figure had grown to 236 billion. Its employees worked hard to handle this growing business more efficiently. Average tons per train increased from 5,533 in 2001 to 5,719 in 2004. Revenue per employee increased from $206,000 in 2001 to $232,000 in 2004.

As it entered the fifth year of independence, CPR kept its focus on the future. Recognizing that its western business would continue to grow, in early 2005 it announced a $160 million capital investment program in

CP SD90MAC/43 units 9127 and 9120 are at the head end of westbound Train 493 (a Toronto–Vancouver double-stack) at Kicking Horse Pass on the Laggan Subdivision in September 1999. Photographer John Leopard notes that, "this photo was taken on the 'new' second main line built on the eastern slope of Kicking Horse Pass. The new track is 5.5 miles (8.9 kilometers) long, was built between Lake Louise and Stephen (on the Continental Divide) at a cost of $14 million, and was completed in May 1981. This track became the westward main track with a ruling grade of 1.0 percent, bypassing the original main's gradient of up to 1.8 percent. The original line became the eastward track." *John Leopard*

At 9,138 feet (2,785 meters) Crowsnest Mountain towers above this westbound train as it skirts the shore of Crowsnest Lake west of Coleman, Alberta, in September 1999. *John Leopard*

western Canada, including 22 projects to extend sidings and install sections of double-track between Vancouver, Calgary, and Moose Jaw. The improvements, CPR said, would give it 12 percent more line capacity between Calgary and Vancouver, which would be used to accommodate increases in intermodal, coal, potash, and other bulk commodity traffic.

CPR's Place on the North American Rail Map

Looking ahead, there is every reason to believe that CPR can continue as a self-sustaining, independent company, able to continue financing the improvements it will need to handle future traffic growth.

The only uncertainty hanging over the company involves factors outside its control, specifically, the structure of the North American rail-freight industry. From time to time,

talk surfaces about future mergers among the six largest railways (four U.S. and two Canadian). Unlike any of the other six, CPR has not participated in a major merger or consolidation in recent history; today it is the smallest of the "big six." With an east–west orientation in an increasingly north-south economy, can CP determine its own fate or will its limited geographic reach in the United States make it an acquiree, rather than an acquirer?

CPR's management and employees would, no doubt, vote to maintain the company's legacy as the railway that created Canada. At the 125th anniversary of its incorporation, CPR is a strong, independent, and growing company. That fact is a testament to the hard work of its people, who deserve to be as proud of their accomplishments as earlier generations—those who built, expanded, and strengthened the company—were of theirs.

SOURCES

Books

Berton, Pierre. *The Impossible Railway: The Building of the Canadian Pacific.* New York: Alfred A. Knopf, 1972.

——.*The Last Spike: The Great Railway, 1881–1885.* Toronto: McClelland and Stewart, 1971.

——.*The National Dream: The Great Railway, 1871–1881.* Toronto: McClelland and Stewart, 1970.

Buck, George. *From Summit to Sea: An Illustrated History of Railroads in British Columbia and Alberta.* Calgary: Fifth House Ltd., 1997.

Burrows, Roger G. *Railway Mileposts: British Columbia, Volume I: The CPR Mainline Route From the Rockies to the Pacific Including the Okanagan Route and CN's Canyon Route.* North Vancouver, B.C.: Railway Milepost Books, 1981.

——.*Railway Mileposts: British Columbia, Volume II: The Southern Routes from the Crowsnest to the Coquihalla.* North Vancouver, B.C.: Railway Milepost Books, 1984.

Cruise, David, and Alison Griffiths. *Lords of the Line: The Men Who Built the CPR.* Markham, Ont.: Viking, 1988.

Dean, Murray W., and David B. Hanna. *Canadian Pacific Diesel Locomotives.* Toronto: Railfare Enterprises Limited, 1981.

Dubin, Arthur D. *More Classic Trains.* Milwaukee, Wis.: Kalmbach Publishing Co., 1974.

Garden, J. F. *The Crow and the Kettle: The CPR in Southern British Columbia and Alberta 1950–1989.* Cowley, Alta.: Footprint Publishing Co. Ltd., 2004.

——.*Nicholas Morant's Canadian Pacific.* Revelstoke, B.C.: Footprint Publishing, 1991.

The Historical Guide to North American Railroads. Waukesha, Wis.: Kalmbach Books, 2000.

Hyde, Frederick W. *Soo Line 1993 Review.* Denver: Hyrail Productions, 1993.

Lamb, W. Kaye. *History of the Canadian Pacific Railway.* New York: MacMillan Publishing, 1977.

Lavallée, Omer. *Canadian Pacific Steam Locomotives.* Toronto: Railfare Enterprises Limited, 1985.

——.*Van Horne's Road: An Illustrated Account of the Construction and First Years of Operation of the Canadian Pacific Transcontinental Railway.* Montreal: Railfare Enterprises Limited, 1974.

Linley, Bill. *Canadian Pacific in Color, Vol. 1: Eastern Lines.* Scotch Plains, N.J.: Morning Sun Books, 2003.

McDonnell, Greg. *Canadian Pacific: Stand Fast, Craigellachie!* Erin, Ont.: Boston Mills Press, 2003.

——.*The History of Canadian Railroads.* London: New Burlington Books, 1985.

McDougall, J. Lorne. *Canadian Pacific: A Brief History.* Montreal: McGill University Press, 1968.

McKee, Bill, and Georgeen Klassen. *Trail of Iron: The CPR and the Birth of the West.* Vancouver: Douglas & McIntyre Ltd., 1983.

Pole, Graeme. *The Spiral Tunnels and the Big Hill: A Canadian Railway Adventure.* Canmore, Alta.: Altitude Publishing Canada Ltd., 1995.

Sanford, Barrie. *The Pictorial History of Railroading in British Columbia.* Vancouver: Whitecap Books Ltd., 1981.

Turner, Robert D. *Sternwheelers and Steam Tugs: An Illustrated History of the Canadian Pacific Railway's British Columbia Lake and River Service.* Victoria, B.C.: Sono Nis Press, 1998.

——.*Vancouver Island Railroads.* San Marino, Calif.: Golden West Books, 1973.

——.*West of the Great Divide: An Illustrated History of the Canadian Pacific Railway in British Columbia 1880–1986.* Winlaw, B.C.: Sono Nis Press, 2003.

Zuters, Gary. *CP Rail 1993 Review.* Ferndale, Wash.: Hyrail Productions, 1994.

Other Publications

Lavallée, Omer, and Robert R. Brown. "Locomotives of the Canadian Pacific Railway Company." *Railroad History,* Issue 83, July 1981.

Moody's Investors Service, *Manual of Investments: Railroad Securities,* various editions.

——.*Transportation Manual,* various editions.

The Official Guide of the Railways, various issues. New York: National Railway Publication Company.

Canadian Pacific Railway and Canadian Pacific Limited Materials

Annual reports, various years.

Canadian Pacific Facts and Figures. Montreal: Canadian Pacific Foundation Library, 1946.

Investor fact books, 2000–2004.

Maps and travel brochures.

Public and employee timetables.

Other Resources

Canadian Pacific Line (steamships) Web site, http://www.theshipslist.com/ships/lines/cp.html

Canadian Pacific Railway Web site, http://www.cpr.ca

Canadian Pacific Railway Archives Web site, http://www.cprheritage.com

Canadian Railway Hall of Fame Web site, http://railfame.ca

Ehrlich, Leslie, and Bob Russell, "Employment Security and Job Loss: Lessons from Canada's National Railways, 1956–1995," *Labour/Le Travail,* Spring 2003, http://www.historycooperative.org/journals/llt/51/ehrlich.html

Old Time Trains Web site (R. L. Kennedy), http://www.trainweb.org/oldtimetrains

Rothstein, Tracey, "A History of Western Canadian Grain Rates 1897–1984," *Manitoba History,* Number 18, Autumn 1989, http://www.mhs.mb.ca/docs/mb_history/18/grainrates.shtml

INDEX